CHANGING CHANNELS

The Church and the Television Revolution

Edited by Tyron Inbody

WHALEPRINTS™

DAYTON, OHIO

First Edition

Published in the United States of America.
Whaleprints ™
1810 Harvard Boulevard
Dayton, Ohio 45406-4599

Library of Congress Catalog Card Number: 90-91405

ISBN: 1-882122-00-3

CONTENTS

This book is dedicated to our colleagues at United Theological Seminary whose openness to emerging electronic forms of communication signals hope for the church in a new media era.

FOREWORD

Martin E. Marty

In the days of the Second Vatican Council, St. Louis University President Paul C. Reinert, S.J., was once overheard expressing jealousy. As a university president, he said, he sometimes envied the Pope: it was much easier to reform the five hundred million member Catholic Church than it was to reform a five-member university social science department.

Ironies abound in the situation which finds institutions of higher learning less mobile than others when it comes to self-criticism and reform. Their faculties are made up of experts at suspicion; their social scientists learn to train their eyes on the entrenchments and resistances of all agencies beyond the academy. Yet the inability of academics to be effective when they engage in basic critiques of their own social forms is proverbial. So is their ability to be "dug in," to defend their old and own ways of doing things. Perhaps it takes higher learning to learn how to put such high investment in the *status quo* even when the stakes are relatively low. Academics get good at defending what they do not want reformed.

At least some of them do. I should know. I am one of them.

Along with most people in the higher academic study of religion and, at the margins, in theological and ministerial education, I have mistrust of most of what has happened in the "electronic revolution." My colleagues and I can effect appropriate sneers, or can find them coming naturally, at almost all religious uses of radio and television to present religion or, in many of our cases, the Christian faith. Most of us can find convenient ways of postponing or permanently pushing aside the notion that we might have to change because virtually all humans in range of electricity have changed their modes of grasping reality in this century, thanks to the invention of tubes and batteries and chips and screens.

Such academic conservatism has its place. That radio, the cinema, and television can be destructive of humane purpose is such an obvious reality that it would induce nothing but boredom if we set out to document the proposition. The notion of "going with the flow," "riding the trend," or adopting something new because it is new ill befits institutions, disciplines, or scholars dedicated to creative foot-dragging in the face of fashions and fads. But now and then it is important to be suspicious about suspicion.

1

This book, on its negative side, is precisely that. Its intended audience is first of all professional, as the editor makes clear. The professions involved include ministry, religious education, church leadership, opinion-formation and mass communications. The primary focus is on institutions devoted to theological education and those which benefit or suffer from the ripple-effect of such institutions. While in the narrower sense this seems to be aimed at only a couple score thousand people, in the broader sense it affects millions, part of whose spiritual life at least is influenced by people in those professions.

Theological schools, says the gentle but persistent critique that runs through these chapters, have shown a singular lack of imagination when it comes to conceiving, appraising and addressing issues raised by the electronic media in respect to religion. But if this book were nothing but one more crabby attack on technology and media in the name of humane and Christian values, it would belong on the shelves where dust has been gathering for decades on works of the attacking nature.

Instead this is largely a positive and eventually programmatic work. It diagnoses only enough to begin to present its address to therapy. Most of the pages are attempts at seeing how different things could be. It is embarrassing to have to call a work of 1990 on this subject "pioneering," but it may be worth a blush to do so for the sake of honesty. While one does not picture a flow of thank-you cards to United Theological Seminary for choosing to amass resources and put energies into this field of inquiry and while one cannot picture drastic and instant reform of theological education -- remember the Reinert observation -- one must have at least as much realistic hope as these almost optimistic contributors of chapters that the beginning of the beginning of a turn could come before this century's end.

Invited late to the United Theological Seminary party to write this Foreword, I find it necessary to lay my credentials on the host table. Reading these essays gave me occasion to revisit for the first time after thirty years -- **thirty years!** -- my *The Improper Opinion: Mass Media and the Christian Faith* (Westminster, 1961), a book occasioned by a series editor's interest in response to the transformation of life caused by the intrusion of television in the previous dozen years. I found myself still believing what that book asserted: that, on the negative side, "the Protestant imagination" was not ready for television and, on the positive side, when not only Protestants but Christians at large would make effective use of the media, they would find the method of "indirection" most congruent with the gospel. The cross of Jesus Christ is somehow misfit in the fitting worlds of mass opinion.

What that book did not address or, frankly, envision, was the way hardline and enthusiastic religion -- fundamentalism, evangelicalism, Pentecostalism, conservative and charismatic Catholicism -- would seize at least some channels and score with "direct" communication. I could myself turn crabby at this point and engage in theological critique of the distortions of the Christian gospel which have ordinarily accompanied such use, but that would not be in place here because that is not what this book is about. These chapters are not saying: "Imitate the success-mongers." They are summoning the Catholic, Orthodox, Anglican, mainstream Protestant, and most serious evangelical worlds -- the latter of which also having been less successful with television -- to discern their **own** genius and find means of expressing it. Each should ask what in their understanding of the gospel gives them eyes to see and ears to hear and then to find discernment, imagination and energy to do something about addressing publics shaped largely by the mass media.

On one hand, the authors express great interest in being faithful to the tradition of the Christian faith. In that sense, they are conservative. But it would also be hard to overestimate the radicalism of what they venture: to take a fresh look at the problems and possibilities posed by television and then to reform theological education and church thinking and acting so that in the future there would be a more positive use of the medium. While they are critical of colleagues who express "knee-jerk" negative reactions to the medium and their kind of endeavor, fortunately they spend little time expressing that criticism. Most of the endeavor is positive and rich in proposal.

One of the authors has difficulty picturing translating the ponderous systems of Karl Barth, Paul Tillich or Rudolf Bultmann, theological giants of the century, to television. That is one of the rare places in the book where I think they underestimate possibilities. Of course, the translation would have to be drastic and wrenching, but it needs not be unfaithful. I believe that what those titans talked about was an address to the human condition in the light of a Word or the New Being that is so appropriate it can be translated. Many of the great dramas and films of the era were secular versions of such an address, and they reached popular audiences. Of course, such an address on television would not attract as large an audience as do or did the "Abundant Life" kinds of programs which offered so much material profit to the tuner-in, donor, or devotee. But it might find an audience of people who now dismiss religion and Christianity itself because they know about it chiefly by negative reference to disgraced televangelists.

No one in the book sets out to undercut the basic notions of rhetoric or Christian proclamation. They know the need for a *logos*,

3

a word to be spoken; for the *ethos* or character of the communicating agent; for the *pathos* which leads to identification with the needs and interests of the potential viewer. They simply have more faith than do most of us in the possibility that television can be an instrument for meeting such needs, as books do for some and did for many when the printed page represented the communications revolution.

I won't waste a moment saying what these authors say, since they are perfectly capable of stating their own cases. This is simply the place to thank United Theological Seminary, the Lily Endowment, the editor and contributors, for nudging us into new states of uncomfortability about a set of changes which threaten to leave behind many serious forms of Christianity, and for projecting visions and programs for bringing about change. Of course, as Father Reinert might predict, we will "dig in" and resist. But theological education has changed before and perhaps, thanks to efforts like this, it might position itself better to change again. And if it does and there is a better use of television in respect to Christian faith, it just might be that something the critics of television hoped for might come about: a more humane address to the human condition and what Christians conceive that a judging, grace-full God has in store for effecting change. Call it "salvation."

The Divinity School
The University of Chicago
Chicago, Illinois

PREFACE

One of the upheavals of the twentieth century has been the development of several new electronic media. Television is one of the omnipresent and most influential of these innovations.

Some conservative evangelical churches eagerly have adopted this medium for the presentation of the gospel, particularly in the form of the "electronic church." Roman Catholics have begun to adapt their educational methods to this medium. Mainline Protestant churches and the academy, however, continue to be primarily critical of the medium or at least skeptical about its use as a medium appropriate for their work.

This book grew out of a project sponsored by the Lilly Foundation. Several faculty of United Theological Seminary decided not to dismiss television with the typical knee-jerk reaction of most clergy and academics. Instead, they confronted the question of the use of television by the churches and seminaries with a more open-minded and analytical perspective. The result is a book written by representatives of the mainline churches and seminaries which calls for a more positive appraisal of the prospects of television as a user-friendly medium for the mainline Protestant churches.

Each author is deeply committed to the church and represents a teaching discipline within the church's academy. Each inquires into the church's use of television with two questions in mind. First, what distinctive insight into the problems of understanding the church's use of television can my scholarly expertise contribute? Each approaches the possibility of the appropriation of television in some specific aspect of the church's life. Second, what considered judgments can I offer the church as it pursues this discussion in the twenty-first century?

From the beginning of the project these two questions guided the discussion of the participants. Inaugurated in 1988 as a formal faculty study, the project proceeded through deliberate stages. Seven faculty of United from diverse scholarly fields -- church history, biblical studies, theology, religious education, communications, mission and evangelism -- agreed to participate in a two year study of electronic media guided by the two questions. After the participants met to outline the project, each prepared a seminar paper to present to the entire faculty during a series of Friday afternoon colloquies. The essays subsequently were rewritten in the light of critical responses offered during the colloquies. Finally, Gregor Goethals, Professor of Art History and Director of Graduate Studies at the Rhode Island School of Design, and Quentin Schultze, Professor of Communication Arts and Sciences at Calvin College, joined the project as outside consultants to help reshape the chapters into final form. The papers of this two year project are contained in this volume.

The distinctiveness of this book is that the writers, intentionally representing both the church and the academy, carve out new territory for the conversation. All believe it is time for the assumptions of the two extremes -- uncritical adaptation and uncritical rejection -- to be examined with more discrimination. The deliberate stance can be described as "critical openness." The authors are "critical" because they are willing to examine the assumptions about television from each side of the debate. But they are also "open" because they are willing to explore without preconceived conclusions, guided only by preferences or prejudices, the possibilities of the church's employment of new electronic media for carrying out its mission.

The common arguments that emerge, and that represent the themes which make them a coherent whole, are first: there are no compelling grounds to conclude that television is not an appropriate medium for several aspects of the church's ministry, and second: there are good reasons to believe that television is an appropriate medium for the mission of a church which is both postmodern and faithful to its message. The authors intend to inaugurate a new phase of the discussion by eschewing both reactionary negativism, which is often a religious version of academic elitism, and cheerleader optimism, which is too often a religious version of the hucksterism of Sinclair Lewis's George Babbitt or Elmer Gantry. Each author is convinced that a unique blend of "critical openness" is the distinctive contribution a theological school faculty can make to discussion about the use of television by the church.

The ferment for the examination was provided early on by Thomas Boomershine, who has devoted much of his teaching career to exploring the questions. Through two papers delivered to the faculty within a period of three years, "Christianity in Ancient and Modern Media" (1982), and "Theological Education and Media" (1985), he introduced the use of television to the agenda of the seminary. When Leonard Sweet came to United Theological Seminary in 1985 as President, he saw the implications of a medium shift for the future of theological education. His vision, administrative commitment and enthusiasm for exploring the import of an electronic age for the church and for theological education provided the initiative to get the project off the ground. He has supported the faculty at each step along the way.

The research would not have been possible without the grant from the Lilly Foundation to underwrite the program. The Lilly Foundation has been visionary over the years in its support of creative directions in theological education. The book is the final product of the faculty participation in a more comprehensive project in electronic media studies at United sponsored by Lilly.

Acclaim must go to the faculty who participated in the deliberation. Most readers of this book probably do not know how novel it is for a high percentage of any theological school faculty to be involved directly in any common study which moves beyond the borders of their research specialization. United is a unique school in this respect, and is itself the hint of what a postmodern seminary will look like in the willingness of faculty to transcend the rigid boundaries of the modern theological school curriculum. Newell Wert, Vice President for Academic Affairs and Dean, supported the project from its inception through its various stages, both by helping to administer the faculty participation and by participating himself as an eager partner in the discussion.

The authors are introduced to the reader informally in two places. Through transcribed oral interviews edited for print, the writers offer some insight into their distinctive interests, perspective and style. First, in the Contributors' list following the Preface, each author suggests what "totem bird or animal" best expresses their understanding of themselves as person, teacher and scholar. Then this self-description is continued at the beginning of each chapter where the writers present their spontaneous responses to such questions posed by the editor as: Do you watch a lot of television? Do you feel guilty about watching television? If you had an unlimited budget to produce television programs, what would you produce? How does television affect your teaching and how does your work as a scholar and teacher affect your view of television?

The editor owes a large debt to many individuals who contributed to this project. Most obvious and immediate is my debt to Thelma Monbarren, Director of Public Relations at United, who devoted countless hours of technical knowledge and skills in another electronic medium, the microcomputer, to produce text and graphics. Betty O'Brien, Research Assistant, produced the Index. Thelma, Betty and JoAnn Gilmore, Administrative Assistant in the Doctor of Ministry Program, read proofs at one stage or another of the project.

My two sons have contributed more to my perspective on television than they know. Mark, the older one, proved to me that not everyone today is primarily a product of our television culture. And David, the younger one, showed me that some who are deeply

7

shaped by television are understanding and humane persons.

Finally, but not least, I want to express gratitude to my wife, Fran, who asked me at the very beginning of the project how I could justify working on a book which, ironically, would advocate the importance of media other than print. My answer was strictly academic and not very compelling. She is herself an excellent teacher with an innate sense of complementary styles of thinking and ways of learning through several media. If other professors and writers had access to the grace of balance and perspective I have in her, their work would undoubtedly be even more interesting and satisfying.

CONTRIBUTORS

Quentin J. Schultze (Ph.D., University of Illinois, Urbana-Champaign, 1978) is Professor of Communication Arts and Sciences at Calvin College. His books include *American Evangelicals and the Mass Media* (1990) and *Television: Manna from Hollywood?* (1986). His articles have appeared in numerous newspapers, magazines, and scholarly journals, including *Critical Studies in Mass Communications*.

"I think I am a fox in the sense that I am a sort of hit-and-run teacher and scholar. I race in before people even see that I am there, grab the food -- some idea or theory or perspective -- eat it and hand it out in a kind of foxy communion to my students and readers. Then I'm immediately off to another victim, very fast, very sly, with great forethought, but mainly invisible."

James D. Nelson (Ph.D., University of Chicago, 1963) is Professor of Church History at United Theological Seminary. He is translator and editor of *The Life of Jacob Albright* (forthcoming). Recent essays have appeared in *Religious Studies Review, UTS Journal of Theology,* and *Wesleyan Spirituality in Contemporary Theological Education.* He has contributed numerous entries to the *Encyclopedia Britannica* and the *Westminster Dictionary of Church History.*

"As an historian I am like a big horn sheep. If you are in the mountains and you look around, on some far peak a big horn sheep is going to be watching you. He is interested in what you are doing. But there is distance. Distance is somewhat lost in the immediacy of television. How do you maintain the distance? How do you get the unblinking gaze that enables you to obtain some semblance of a true picture then that can be made into meaning? I can't stop being an historian when I watch television. I'm often conscious of what the editors are doing in the news."

Thomas E. Boomershine (Ph.D., Union Theological Seminary, 1974) is Professor of New Testament at United Theological Seminary. His book on storytelling, *Story Journey: An Introduction to the Gospel as Storytelling*, appeared in 1988, and chapters have appeared in *Urban Church Education, Apocalyptic and the New Testament*, and *Religious Education and Telecommunications* and articles in *Journal of Biblical Literature* and *Semeia*.

"I realized about three years ago, in the context of a kind of spiritual analysis of different types of people, that my totem animal is the deer. It has become my new totem -- strong, fast, fleet, overcoming all kinds of barriers, but also very accessible and gentle."

Tyron Inbody (Ph.D., University of Chicago, 1973) is Professor of Theology at United Theological Seminary. He is editor of the *UTS Journal of Theology*. Articles and chapters have appeared recently in *Zygon, Perspectives in Religious Studies, American Journal of Theology and Philosophy, Process Studies*, and *God, Values and Empiricism*.

"If I were an animal or bird, I would choose to be an eagle. It's not a safe choice. From a distance you can't tell the difference between an eagle and a vulture. An eagle is a high flying bird which is able to see the big, comprehensive picture. It has good eyes for viewing far distances and for spotting the specific, the concrete, in great detail. The eagle eye encompasses the minute and the magnificent at the same time. It knows both the universal and the concrete. To see and enjoy the concrete and to be able to think about it abstractly are not contradictory or even dialectical. The full reality is both the general and the specific. My views of God, theology, the church, popular culture and even myself increasingly are shaped by this holism."

Pamela Mitchell (Ed.D, Presbyterian School of Christian Education, 1986) is Assistant Professor of Christian Education and Communications at United Theological Seminary. Her dissertation was on "Curriculum for Religious Education: A Kierkegaardian Reconceptualization. She has published a chapter in *Small Church Ministry*, and articles in *Religious Education Journal* and the *UTS Journal of Theology* on Kierkegaard. Other research and teaching interests include film criticism.

"My totem animal is a blind mole rat. It reminds me of a quote in an article one of my colleagues required his class to read: 'When In Trouble, When In Doubt, Run In Circles, Scream and Shout.' I first saw these blind mole rats at the Cincinnati Zoo and was absolutely entranced. They were running mazes all over the place. They couldn't see where they were going. But they ran intricate patterns and found things and picked up things and changed directions and kept going all sorts of different ways. I could have stood there for hours watching them. They are really ugly, too. They get where they are going, but they don't go the shortest distance between two points."

Kenneth Bedell (Ph.D. candidate, Temple University) is Director of Computer Ministries at United Theological Seminary. His graduate work in sociology focuses on the sociological understanding of the role of technology. His books include *Worship in the Methodist Tradition* (1976) and *The Role of Computers in Religious Education* (1986). In addition he has published articles in *Review of Religious Research*, *International Bulletin of Missionary Research*, and *Computers in the Church*.

"The animal that comes to mind immediately that describes me and my work is the sparrow. The sparrow keeps going around collecting things and putting them in places where people don't want to have them. People keep tossing them out, and the sparrow keeps collecting these things together and trying to make something out of the place that has already been established, like a garage or an exhaust fan. But the sparrow persists in making a home or a well-constructed nest there. A sparrow leaves some of itself there, puts his own body on the line. And that's what I do in my work with the various electronic media."

Norman E. Thomas (Ph.D., Boston University, 1968) is Vera B. Blinn Professor of World Christianity at United Theological Seminary. He is book editor of *Missiology: An International Review*, and has published basic bibliographies in Ecumenics, Evangelism, and Missions. He has a chapter in *Three Worlds of Christian-Marxist Encounters* (1985), and articles in *Missiology*, *International Bulletin of Missionary Research*, *Mission Studies*, and *Journal of Church and State*.

"My animal is a border collie. Not in its present domesticated form, but in its original purpose, which is sheep-herding in the highlands of Scotland. They work in rugged terrain, the mountains where you are on an edge and you choose that frontier purposefully. When I came to United Theological Seminary, it was the first time I had ever candidated for a position. This position was on a frontier, and I want my work to be on the frontiers. Nobody else wanted to do it. The scholarship that I am doing, particularly the bibliographic work, is something you have to plug away at and constantly devote time to on a systematic and scrupulous basis. For the border collie it is a concern for the preservation and care of the flock. The focus of my work is very much the same -- the community of faith: concern for it and care of it. That takes a lot of running."

Donald B. Rogers (Ph.D., Princeton Theological Seminary, 1967) is Professor of Christian Education at United Theological Seminary. His recent books include *Urban Church Education* and *Teachable Moments*. He has published articles in *Religious Education* and the *UTS Journal of Theology*.

"I'm working on a coyote theology. Coyotes are survivors, gentle survivors. They are part of the trickster tradition, which has dimensions of Native American and many other religions. The coyote is a character that is not always eagerly sought after, except by those who wish to save their poor sheep from slaughter. Coyotes have some very nice, gentle characteristics as a survivor, such as a stern family setup. They pick out one of the litter to stay and help raise the next litter. All the others have to get out. This sounds strange in our day and age when our kids are always coming back. Coyotes are also territorial; they stay put. Part of the benefit is that they are solitary. That is why they spread so rapidly. But they also are omnivorous. They will live on what's there--berries, carrion, what they can kill."

INTRODUCTION:

COKE BOTTLES, OXEN AND UTOPIAS

Tyron Inbody

Can the church sing, pray, preach and teach on television? The question is reminiscent of Israel's exilic lament, "How can we sing the Lord's song in a foreign land?" The juxtaposition of the images of the television set and the church serves as a metaphor for a larger set of questions facing the church in the twenty-first century. How will the church adapt to a postmodern culture dominated by electronic media? Can the church change to an electronic channel as another passageway through which to carry out its commission?

THE ELECTRONIC COKE BOTTLE

During an interview on NBC's "The Today Show" on April 28, 1989, George Gerbner, Dean of the Annenberg School of Communications at the University of Pennsylvania, called television "the new religion, the new environment into which our children are born." Regardless of whether or not the web of public meanings spun by the vernacular of television constitutes a new religion, television is both a primary medium and an omnipresent symbol of a new culture. Television serves both as the most pervasive sign in our world today of electronic culture and as a specific medium through which to explore its significance.

The church continues to represent some characteristics of an oral culture in the contemporary world, most obviously in the preaching in ethnic churches and the churches of the cultural right, but also in the liturgical and parish life of all congregations. In other respects, however, the more modern the church has become the more deeply committed it has been to print culture. The form of the printed page has profoundly shaped the way the church thinks, the content of its thinking, and its educational programs.

The emergence of electronic media in the twentieth century has confounded the church. Like the Coke bottle dropped from the airplane into the preliterate culture of the Kalahari Desert in *The Gods Must Be Crazy*, or the ringing in the ears of Adela Quested which began when East met West in the Marabar Caves in *Passage to India*, the church has become disoriented by the appearance of these mysterious media -- electronic Coke bottles and ringing noises -- which do not fit easily into our modern way of perceiving, interpreting and responding to the world. The church, whether liberal or conservative, is attempting to interpret the gospel in the modern world, and the modern world is being transformed before our eyes and ears into a postmodern world. Electronic media in general, and television in particular, are both token and vehicle of this new era.

Most liberal church pastors and the academy have been negative in their evaluation of the electronic media. Their thought, well-considered or not, is that either the electronic media or those who employ it represent intellectual shallowness, moral insensitivity, commercial exploitation, spiritual bankruptcy and aesthetic barrenness. At the other end of the religious spectrum, many of the conservative churches have adopted with an uncritical eye the use of the electronic media. They assume these media are merely one more technology given by God to proclaim the gospel near the end times. Because the field is ripe for harvest, these new media should be exploited with little concern about the intellectual, moral, commercial and aesthetic implications.

Throughout these eight chapters, common purposes, themes and conclusions emerge among the participants. These never reach the status of settled conclusions. They are clear enough, however, that they can be offered to the church and the academy as hypotheses for further research and conversation.

ECCLESIASTICAL AND ACADEMIC DOUBTERS

The first reality the leaders of the church and the seminaries have to face in examining television as a medium for ministry is their own innate disposition against electronic culture. In part this bias is based on the fact that the professional and personal identity of leaders depends on their mastery of print culture. No one earns a masters or doctoral degree without mastering books and discursive thinking. The modes of perception and appreciation characteristic of electronic media appear as an "alien nation" to those at home in the land of books and leisurely discussion.

In part the fear of electronic media is based on a more general suspicion of popular culture. The leadership of the established churches and of the seminaries, despite public commitment to ministry to those outside an educated elite, has an innate distrust of anything popular or what the "average" person can understand and appreciate. If television provides the vernacular of our popular culture today -- a web of meanings nearly everyone can understand and share in common -- television is the natural object of scorn for the educated elite. The extent to which church leaders and seminary professors go to reassure their colleagues that they do not watch much television, or if they do they watch only "quality" television, shows how intrinsic this inclination against popular culture is to the personal and professional self-understanding of church leaders.

Closely allied with the personal issues provoked by the appearance of new media is the assumption of many policy makers that the electronic media are inherently biased against tradition as such, or at least certain traditions of the church, such as the exegetical, theological, liturgical and pedagogical heritage of the modern church. The truth of this assumption is not self-evident. It may be false or at least extreme. It is possible, of course, that some of these traditions are so skewed against electronic forms of perception and expression that they are bound to be marginalized or even eclipsed if electronic forms come to dominate the church. But this cannot be taken as a settled conclusion. What needs to be explored more openly is the possibility that electronic media may be a new way, perhaps a superior way, to re-enter memory, and that some of the specific traditions of the church may be re-invented by adopting and adapting to new media.

MEDIUM AS TECHNOLOGY AND INSTITUTION

The term "electronic medium" conveys the union of electronic technology and social institution. There are two extreme views that can characterize the discussion of television as technology and institution. Both misrepresent the actual situation by neglecting an essential ingredient in every electronic medium.

One extreme view is that television is a new technology which exists independent of the social uses made of it. As a novel way of coordinating the eye and ear, image and sound, the medium itself shapes the ways its users apprehend the world independent of the conscious intent of those who develop it and those who consume it. Such "technological determinism" implies that regardless of the intentions of producer and consumer, the medium itself so skews the balance of eye and ear that the world must be perceived in ways radically different from what is characteristic of other media. There are some ways the world cannot be seen in an electronic medium, and there are other ways one inevitably sees the world through it. It is the technology itself, and not the malevolent or benevolent aims and efforts of its users, that determine discernment. Any discussion of the church's use of the medium that is not informed by what the medium can and must do to its users is perilous. Either the church will not be able to convey what it intends to convey because the medium is incapable of it, or it will convey something different from what it intends because the medium will shape producer and consumer alike according to the laws and jaws of the technology.

At the other extreme is "sociological determinism." Its advocates argue that the questions of who uses the medium and how they use it are the primary considerations in understanding television. The medium itself is simply a benign tool. The question at issue in understanding television is its social significance, namely, its capacity to reflect the values and purposes of those who use it. Some social group with its own aims and interests inevitably controls how the medium is used. Although it is exploited in our culture today primarily by the dominant cultural and economic groups to expand and protect their vested interests, it could be employed for other purposes by other groups. "It's only how you use the tool that counts," and if the church decides to utilize this new medium to tell its story, teach its perspective and work for justice, it can use this neutral tool for redeeming instead of abusive purposes.

The truth is that television is a medium. It is a dynamic interaction between a new technology and institutions. It is a grand boulevard laid out through the center of our global village which combines several technologies and can be traveled by many groups for a variety of purposes. The issue is more than how the user uses the tool. The issue is also how the user is used by the technology. Media both shape and reflect the values and interests of the culture in which they are used, especially the mythic, informational, political and economic authority of the groups which dominate the web of meaning expressed in the medium.

ECCLESIASTICAL AND ACADEMIC OXEN

If the first two points about doubt and medium are correct, one can more easily understand why the leaders of the church and the academy are cautious about moving into another medium with any eagerness and ease. Whose ox is being gored? Whose interests are threatened if electronic media significantly begin to supplement or even to supplant the dominance of the print media? Primary representatives of several institutions have vested interests in the well-established media. But no group today has more invested in the maintenance of print culture than the academy, including divinity schools and theological seminaries. Church leaders and academic leaders in part are tempted to block or to reject new media in order to preserve their hard earned authority in our culture. By keeping the church dependent on print culture as one of the primary media for understanding and preservation of Christian faith, the academy helps to maintain its authority.

There is nothing cynical in the acknowledgement that ideology plays a role in the thought of everyone. All the authors in this book believe that the printed word and rational discourse are crucial to the future of the church in a postmodern culture. To acknowledge the role of vested interest is not to concede that every defense of oral and print culture is nothing but ideology. It is to try to eliminate any strictly ideological arguments from the agenda of both church and academy by making self-deception more difficult. Power -- political, economic and intellectual -- will clearly be redistributed as dominant media and control of them shift. Recognition of the role of ideology in one's analysis and evaluation of our cultural shift is not paralyzing. Rather, it frees the church and the academy to ask a wider range of questions about the new medium.

THE CRUNCHING EFFECTS

When the gospel is presented through a particular medium, whether that medium be oral, manuscript, print or electronic, the content of the gospel is reshaped by the medium. The tradition is "crunched," or the message goes through a "useful mutilation" as it is transmitted through a particular technology. Each dimension of the church's life is affected by the shift. Leadership patterns are shifted, exegetical methods are altered, theological meanings are modified and the liturgical, educational and communal life of the church are revised.

For those whose understanding of the gospel has been shaped predominantly by oral and print media, the crunching effects of the electronic media may seem to be an abandonment or distortion of the Christian faith. But that conclusion is not indubitable. The skeptic about the use of television, first of all, must recognize the degree to which his or her own understanding of the "true meaning" of the gospel is dependent on a particular medium. Furthermore, the development of the Christian tradition, including its formation in the earliest years, has been an adaptation and reinterpretation of the message in new cultural forms, including new technologies.

What is needed, and what these chapters offer as a first volley to the church and academic communities, is an understanding of the effects of media on message, and an open mind about the strengths and weaknesses of television as a medium for crunching the church's witness and life.

BETWEEN UTOPIA AND DYSTOPIA

The church and academy would be in a better position both in terms of understanding and of strategy if they stood somewhere between a utopianism based on technological optimism and a dystopianism based on technological pessimism. There are both possibilities for new forms of Christian faith and life in electronic media and risks of distortion and dissipation of faith through an uncritical ca-

17

pitulation to the liabilities of new media.

The church clearly needs a coordinated strategy as it explores the use of television. Program and budget constraints demand a reasonable strategy. But that need cannot be met without a critical and coherent understanding of the new medium and its relation to older media. What television can and cannot do for the transmition of the Christian tradition needs to be understood. What is offered here is an argument that the church and academy must not make a knee-jerk reaction either of adoption or rejection but must understand the new medium and explore possibilities for constructive use. The book is an effort at "consciousness raising" and a strategy of "probing some new possibilities" for the use of television in some concrete aspects of the church's life.

❝ A critical understanding of the electronic media both will allay the fears of the paranoid and caution against utopian optimism. ❞

Without being utopian the writers are optimistic about the possibilities of the church's use of television for its mission. Television is especially promising as a medium for the narrative features of the tradition. Story, drama, docudrama, documentary, dispute, debate and controversy play well on television. The problem is more of vision and of will than of possibility. Too many in the church and the academy have decided prematurely that the medium should be eschewed either as diabolical or unsuitable. That conclusion is a prejudgment unworthy of creative leaders of the church for the twenty-first century or of reflective scholars helping to pilot the church into that century with understanding and confidence.

A critical understanding of the electronic media both will allay the fears of the paranoid and caution against utopian optimism. Our postmodern culture will not be a single medium culture. Television will not replace print as our access to the world and our way of understanding the world. One medium does not supplant another. Media supplement each other. And they complement each other. To some degree each continues to operate with its own integrity as a medium, and to some degree one reshapes the other in novel and unexpected ways.

The norm is appropriateness. Not all media are good for all things. One supports certain modes of perception and styles of thinking better than some others. Insofar as the church and the academy are willing to explore a wide variety of perceptive and cognitive modes for expressing the fullness of Christian faith, the church must explore television as an appropriate medium for Christian faith and life.

THE COMMON TERMS

Throughout this book there appears a number of terms that need to be defined so that the reader knows how the concepts are commonly used by the authors. **Culture** is used in the sociological sense to refer to everything which is socially learned and shared by the members of a society, and includes knowledge, beliefs, art, morals, law, custom and any other capabilities and habits acquired by members of a society. **Mass culture** refers to those elements of culture that are shared by large numbers of people. The term is descriptive and not normative; it distinguishes components of a culture which are shared by a large number of people from those components which are acquired and valued by subgroups within a culture. The opposite of mass is not elite but specialized. **Popular culture** is those elements of culture regarded favorably by people in general as distinguished from those elements regarded with favor by elite or specialized groups in society; the term also applies to beliefs, attitudes or tastes prevailing among masses of people and shared by uneducated and elite alike. Popular culture is a descriptive term and is not to be equated with vulgar culture, which refers to indecent or unrefined.

The term **media** (pl.) refers to agencies, means, methods or instruments by which information is made public. A **mass medium** (sing.) is an instrument which makes information available to a large number of people. These include principally newspapers, magazines, radio, film and television. **Mass media** are forms of communication in which information, ideas, beliefs and attitudes are made available to large numbers of persons who are not individually identified. **Electronic media** are devices, circuits or systems employing electronics, the flow of electrons in a vacuum, in gaseous media and in semiconductors, for means of communication. Electronic media which use the electromagnetic spectrum to communicate include telegraph, telephone, radio, film, audio records and cassettes, television, computers and facsimile machines. In these chapters, unless indicated otherwise, the term refers to the amalgamation of electronic technology and the social institutions which use the technology. Finally, **television** refers to one of the electronic media, namely, the medium in which an electronically produced visual image is coupled to sound and includes network broadcasting, cable, closed circuit, video cassettes, satellites and low power television.

AN INVITATION TO DANCE

These chapters are offered as a stimulus to the reader to participate with the authors in a search they have inaugurated. They are an invitation to engage in research and reflection. Beyond that, though, the book is an invitation to the readers to dance along with the writers as they attempt to move with flexibility and grace into the postmodern culture of the twenty-first century. The mood of these eight teachers is cautious but upbeat. Research and reflection can be pedantic undertakings. They can also be an expression of a new advent of the human spirit undertaken in adventure and expectation. They can exhibit the graceful movement of partners on the dance floor. The book is offered to its readers akin to the challenge between Anna and the King of Siam: "Shall we dance?"

QUENTIN J. SCHULTZE

"Most people in our postmodern culture favor oral and visual forms of communication by virtue of growing up in an electronic age. But the mainline churches are so oriented toward print material that they have failed to see not only the benefits of mass media technologies but the significance of old media like the voice and the ear. The mainline churches have become stylistically irrelevant for growing numbers of people. Preaching tends to be oriented toward a manuscript, presented in a lecture style."

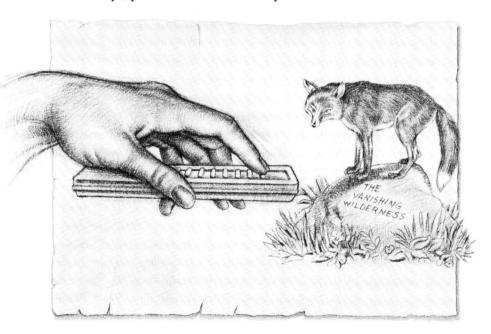

❝ What's badly needed on television is documentaries. I would do very contemporary documentaries, based on the differences individuals and groups are making for the bettering of other people's lives -- a positive, upbeat slant. They would prod the viewer to probe how they could make a difference in the world, rather than provide a means for escaping from the world. ❞

"With every new technology that comes along, people either want to trash it or naively use it. I have always seen my work as taking a baseball bat to the rear ends of those who think new technologies are inherently bad, moving them to do something worthwhile with the technologies, and to take the bat to the heads of those who are naively optimistic and believe that anything you would do with new technology would be inevitably good. My scholarly agenda is to be critical of both groups. I try to find that middle ground where we see the limits of the medium but also the potential. This approach may be somewhat an idiosyncratic reflection of my Calvinism. A good Calvinist should see God's grace in the creation of every new medium and human depravity in the use of it."

"I watch television selectively about an hour a day. In fact, that's the limit in our family. I don't feel guilty about watching it except when it takes me away from more important things, particularly friends and family. There is much good stuff on television if you're willing to poke around for it. You could watch quality television all day, especially cable, public television and video. The problem is that it interferes with living."

"I think the mainline people have done a good job of keeping alive in mass media important political perspectives, social issues and theological concerns. But they have done it in such a dull, prosaic, uninteresting fashion that they have lost out. On the other hand, evangelicals have figured out how to pick up the media and use them in very dramatically powerful ways. Jimmy Swaggart is an incredible performer. No matter what the content of his preaching, he has a kind of dramatic flair and histrionic punch that is simply good television. But the content of what evangelicals have done, almost across the board, is very superficial. They don't have much to say most of the time other than a kind of direct conversion appeal. If you could get the kind of theological and social insights of the mainliners and hook that up with the dramatic flair of the evangelicals, there would be a much larger audience for mainline programs. Also, the programming would be much more engaging."

CHAPTER ONE

THE PLACE OF TELEVISION IN THE CHURCH'S COMMUNICATION

Quentin J. Schultze

The word is so overused these days that we hesitate to call anything a "revolution." If we listen to the advertisers practically every new product is a revolutionary innovation. Or if we believe the popular press and television news programs, it would seem that each day brings revolutions in fashion, politics and economics. A few years ago the cover of *Newsweek*, predicting the death of yuppie life styles, proclaimed the "end of greed." Apparently the editors had a rather limited view of human depravity. More than anything else such loose use of the word "revolution" speaks of our lack of historical insight. Change occurs continuously, but revolutions are hardly everyday occurrences. Revolutions are complete or radical changes, such as the overthrow of governments or the adoption of a new worldview. There is undoubtedly far more continuity than discontinuity in history, and few events or changes should properly be called revolutions.

IS THERE A COMMUNICATIONS REVOLUTION?

We make this observation in the context of the popular use of the term "communications revolution." At least since the 1960s, when media scholar and guru Marshall McLuhan wrote about the impending "global village," the term "revolution" has been widely used to describe changes and developments in the mass media.[1] The word has been applied not only to technological developments, such as the rapid proliferation of the videocassette recorder and cable and satellite communications, but to presumed changes in society and culture as well. In other words, scholars and popular observers alike often assume that new communications technologies produce revolutions in life and thought, work and leisure, values and practices.[2] The phrase "communications revolution" conjures up all kinds of images and sentiments supporting such mythology. Among the most powerful sentiments is the belief that new technologies will necessarily improve the quality of life for people.

Americans are especially prone to celebrate new technologies as signs and symbols of revolutionary improvements in human affairs.[3] There is a long and deep affinity in North America between religious faith and technological optimism.[4] Americans have not only used the term "communications revolution" rather loosely; they have

23

also grafted it to popular religious expression. Part of the appeal of the so-called "televangelists," for example, is the way they infuse religious language with technological rhetoric. Ben Armstrong, Executive Director of National Religious Broadcasters, even interprets scripture through the lens of the technological sublime. He believes that the first angel of Revelation 14 might be a communications satellite proclaiming the gospel from the heavens to the entire world.[5] Armstrong's exegesis also reflects American nostalgia for the past, which is surely one of the great national sicknesses. He favorably compares the new "electric church" with the early household church, and Martin Luther's Protestant revolution with today's religious communications revolution.[6]

But such syntheses of religious faith and technological optimism are not merely the rhetoric of fundamentalists or even evangelicals. Americans of nearly all religions and regions enjoy their technological gadgets and affirm their hope in the always-impending communications revolution. Perhaps only the rural Anabaptists have collectively charted a different course, remaining remarkably separate from the dominant culture of technological celebration.

This chapter examines the extent to which the new communications technologies, especially the electronic media, are really agents of a social or cultural revolution. Moreover, it considers such revolutionary claims primarily in the context of American religious life. Because we are most familiar with American Christianity, we shall limit our observations largely to the Christian faith and to the Christian church in the sense of the "church universal," not in the sense of particular sects, denominations or congregations. Along the way we will make some distinctions between Protestantism and Catholicism as well as between mainline Protestantism and evangelicalism.

Our thesis is that the electronic media will not replace oral and print media, but that all three media forms will exist side by side in the culture. Moreover, we argue that oral, print and electronic media each have distinctive capacities and should all be used appropriately by the church. In the future the strongest religious groups will probably establish an appropriate mix of each media form. Finally, we will suggest that religious educators should serve the church, their own profession and the wider society by addressing in their scholarship and teaching the nature and function of each media form.

Implicit throughout this chapter is the belief that the so-called "revolutionary" effects of the electronic media depend partly on how these media are used, particularly how they are used in conjunction with other media. Either the church will guide the use and effects of the electronic media or, by the church's own inaction, those media will guide the church. The church should not sit idly by, waiting for other social institutions to figure out how to use these media effectively to meet real human needs, especially the needs for community and faith. If the church takes such a wait-and-see attitude, other institutions will largely determine the proper role and purpose for the electronic media in North American society. To some extent that has already happened. Consider the power that commerce and industry already wield over television and radio. For that reason this chapter, like the entire book, is both descriptive and prescriptive. We are not concerned only with the apparent effects of these media on religious faith and practice, but also with the opportunities that the electronic media offer the church for legitimately strengthening itself and enhancing its role in contemporary society.

> **Like symbol-using spiders we are constantly spinning and re-spinning webs of meaning and significance through available communications media.**

Nor should the church charge ahead naively, grabbing every new media technology that comes along. Misguided use of the media might be more spiritually dangerous for American society than no religious use of the media. The church must be careful not to thoughtlessly conform itself to the ways of the world as represented in such things as high ratings and popularity. The church seeks more than to be a witness to the world; it seeks to be an **authentic** witness, reflecting the real joy of the gospel and power of a truly prophetic voice.

All of our technologically related fears and optimism aside, there is undoubtedly a relationship between religion and communications media. To put it more broadly no media are neutral conduits of messages. All media both enable human beings to say, do and think some things while restricting them from saying, doing and thinking other things. Both our ideas and our practices are shaped by available media. As symbol-using, culture-forming creatures, we use communication to fabricate the social environment and re-work the physical environment. As James W. Carey has put it human culture exists in and through communication.[7] Like symbol-using spiders we are constantly spinning and re-spinning webs of meaning and significance through available communications media. This is as true of the sounds of the human voice as it is of the words on the printed page and the images on the television screen. And it is as true of interpersonal communication and local media as it is of national and international ones.

In the context of religion we might say that media both enable and limit beliefs and practices. The scriptures, for example, could not have been preserved easily in one linguistic form for hundreds of years without writing. Although they might have been partly preserved through the kinds of mnemonic devices used in oral cultures, some changes would have been inevitable as the stories and laws were passed on from generation to generation. Written and especially printed communication were significant influences on the shape and content of Christianity, helping the church to spread and even to standardize the faith through canon law. And surely the Protestant emphasis on scripture was not possible without mass-produced, vernacular Bibles. The written and later the printed word objectified religious truth for many people, including today's fundamentalists, who use scripture in ways that would boggle the minds of early Reformers.

Similarly, the electronic media have tended to be conduits for particular religious beliefs and practices, partly because of the kinds of people who use these media and partly because of the inherent nature of electronic media technologies. Televised evangelical religion appears to challenge the beliefs and practices of established churches and denominations, particularly the mainline Protestant and Roman Catholic churches. More than that television seems to be enhancing the status and legitimacy of the spontaneous expressions of religion found among Pentecostals, neo-Pentecostals and charismatics. Is it possible that television communicates particular forms of faith and practice better than others? Will television influence the character of religion as has the written word, especially since the Reformation? Will the new medium perhaps even lead to the formation of broadcast denominations and further erode the mainline church's position in American religious life?

TECHNOLOGY AND INSTITUTION

The difficulty in making claims about the religious bias of media is that all media are simultaneously technologies and social institutions. As technologies the media are equipment, such as cameras, lights, editors and microphones. In this sense the human larynx and ear are technologies, as are pens, typewriters and computers. None of these technologies operate by themselves, however. All of them require people to invent them, to manufacture them, to distribute them and most importantly to use them. Once a media technology is used it necessarily becomes part of a social institution, which further determines what types of communication will be enabled and what types will be restricted.

Oral, print and electronic media all require social institutions as the context for their use. Such social institutions are the values, beliefs and practices that govern the use of a medium. In commercial television, for example, the value placed upon audience ratings largely dictates what types of shows will be aired and which ones will never appear on our sets. Preaching is just as institutionalized as is radio broadcasting or publishing, although we are not inclined to think of it that way. Seminaries teach homiletics and church polity just as universities teach broadcast announcing and regulation. There will always be individual renegades who challenge the ways that particular media are used, but all communications are highly conventional and deeply proscribed and ritualized by particular social institutions. Within some neo-Pentecostal churches today, for example, spontaneity is carefully managed by pastors and elders for the maximum effect, just as some television talk shows manage conflict among guests for the sake of audience ratings.

Every medium is a combination of technology and institution. The biases of the institutions can be changed simply by using the technology in different ways, while those of the technologies cannot be altered, except for the decision not to use them. Media abstinence is always an option, but in the real world new technologies are controlled more by politics and economics than by the willful decisions of individuals.

SPACE AND TIME

Probably the most overlooked bias of media technologies is their inherent effect on how cultures use space and time. Every technology shapes the surrounding culture's temporal sense and spacial location. Oral, print and electronic media all affect culture and organize society differently with respect to space and time. As Harold Adams Innis found in his historical research, these biases at least partly transcend the media's social institutions.[8]

In cultures dependent primarily upon direct, oral communications, cultural and social change are slow through time, but there are great differences across geographic space. Oral cultures, whether in Anabaptist communities or tribal Africa, are oriented toward tradition and highly resistant to change. At the same time their ways of life are normally very different from those in nearby cultures. In some cases there appears to be little or no cultural continuity between oral cultures located on opposite sides of a river, across a canyon or over a mountain. These orally-based cultures are remarkably resilient to change except when they come into contact with other cultures. Then there is usually a gradual process of adaptation and assimilation. However, rarely does one culture completely give way to the other. Both are influenced, even when the less powerful culture is forced coercively to adjust to the ways of the stronger one. Left alone oral cultures are slow to generate new symbols and to innovate novel practices. Their dominant medium, direct speech, largely protects them from the outside world while inhibiting their own transformation into a different culture. Written and especially printed communications change a culture's relationship to space and time. These forms of communication can more easily be preserved temporally while being disseminated geographically. As Innis has suggested the spread of literate culture was part of the growth of national and even international monopolies of knowledge and nation-states. Literate media enabled the development and spread of bureaucracies of all kinds, from governments to businesses and even scientific organizations. Such bureaucracies required the written word to specify and maintain elaborate laws, procedures, penalties and practices, many of the kinds of records now stored digitally in computers and still specified in thick printed volumes.

Religions, too, used the written and later the printed word to expand their influence and standardize their beliefs and practices across geographic space, including oceans. According to Innis imperialism and empire, and the resulting colonization of distant cultures and societies, were necessarily linked to developments in literate communication. These media helped enable the church to evangelize distant cultures, but they also fostered bureaucratic organization and legalistic structures within the church.[9] Today some people leave such denominations in favor of the "simpler," more spontaneous, less restrictive and seemingly more egalitarian ones. Mainline Protestant churches have lost members to evangelical (especially neo-Pentecostal) churches partly because of the latter's open style of worship and non-bureaucratic ecclesiology.

THE IMPACT OF ELECTRONIC MEDIA

The rise of the electronic media, including broadcasting, satellites and cable, probably represents the most significant shift in communications media since the spread of printing. Like the latter electronic media traverse space more easily than does the spoken word. But the electromagnetic spectrum makes distant communications nearly instantaneous, at the speed of light, more rapid even than the pace of sound. Moreover, the two major electronic media, radio and television, do not require literate audiences. They spread more images and sounds to more people more quickly than any other technology. But in so doing they can also dislocate people from their own traditions, conquering space while diminishing cultural continuity with the past. These media often challenge traditional ways of life and older beliefs, promoting the new and the different while breaking with the past. Moreover, the electronic media require less effort on the part of audiences than does the printed word. Reading is simply more physically and mentally taxing than viewing the tube or listening to the radio. Television probably requires less effort even than radio, which demands some imagination, at least for dramatic productions.

Nevertheless, McLuhan's concept of the "global village" was naively simplistic. The electronic media are hardly making the world or even the United States one happy family or one life-sharing community. There still are, and probably always will be, opposing uses for the electronic media: rival religions, competing corporations, factious political groups and embattled nation-states. The electronic media spread messages rapidly, but there has always been resistance and resilience to such messages. Not surprisingly such resistance often comes from cultures and even religions rooted in oral or print media. Scholars often disdain the electronic media's superficial and mindless programming, while fundamentalists challenge the assumed authority of media programmers to dictate public morality.

During the early decades of the twentieth century, regional differences were far more significant in the United States than they are at the close of the same century. Ethnic and racial differences, for example, still exist in some urban and rural areas, but are not nearly as strong. There is far more mobility across religious allegiances as well. Partly because of the impact of electronic media, local ways of life founded on traditional institutions such as the church and the family are generally weaker today than in the past. Oral communication is still important, but it now must compete with both printed and broadcast messages which enter our private spaces, including living rooms and bedrooms.

Parish pastors feel the tug of the electronic church on members of their congregations, just as local teachers realize that television competes for the hearts and minds of their students. Many pastors would prefer that their congregations read religious books rather than watch religious programs because they like the "literate" religious faith more than the one anchored in televised images. In this respect today's mainline pastors have simply inherited the animosity toward "uneducated" preachers that arose in early America with the rapid proliferation of popular and effective itinerant lay evangelists.[10] Oral, print and electronic media produce their own kinds of cultures and sensibilities which become the basis for conflict and mutual criticism.

Today we are living during a period when the electronic media are expanding rapidly in status and significance around the world. Although oral and print media are still vital, broadcasting and narrowcasting are increasingly part of nearly all aspects of society, from Presidential politics to education and religion. As Neil Postman has argued average Americans today probably read less than in previous centuries, but certainly books and periodicals have not disappeared.[11] In fact computers have given birth to thousands of new "desk-top" publishers of books, periodicals and religious and political tracts. Oral communication is similarly alive and well in everything from sales to teaching, although as Kathleen Jamieson has argued, public oratory is not in great shape these days, especially in Presidential politics.[12] Thus, in some respects there is hardly a communications "revolution." The electronic media have not driven other media out of existence. They have simply joined the fray among competing media and among rival groups within society. Broadcasting, for example, in this century became one of the many voices of entertainment, information and persuasion. And the cacophony grows, now with home satellite dishes, fiber optics and even the portable VCR.

MEDIA COMPETITION

However, the electronic media are not benign. Instead of driving out previous media they alter the social and cultural conditions in which all media operate. Along with speech and books we now have radio and television. Each of these media has had to adjust to the arrival of the others. In recent decades nearly all communicators and media have had to consider how to compete with television. Preachers necessarily compete against popular religious writings and broadcasts, all of which seek peoples' attention and interest. Some pastors have responded by creating new church liturgies and worship experiences that stylistically resemble television programs and other popular entertainment. Much of the concern about revitalizing the visual dimension of liturgy is partly a response to the impact of television on congregational expectations and tastes.

Everywhere one turns the competition among media is evident. Newspapers have had to compete with magazines, which have also tried to enter the "television age." Elementary school teachers often say they now have to compete with "Sesame Street" and Saturday-morning cartoons. In short, social institutions which have been dependent primarily on oral or print communications now find that they must change their ways or they will lose considerable status and power in American society. So they either try to revitalize their use of older media or to adopt the newer media, or both. If they refuse such changes, it appears, the electronic age will leave them behind in the ongoing battle for attention and influence.

TELEVISION AND POPULAR RELIGION

Partly because of their bias against tradition, the electronic media have fostered the growth of various kinds of popular religion in the United States. More than the print media they have enabled broadcast preachers and other religious personalities to create invisible "congregations" that exist across geographic space. By building audiences composed of individuals from many different ethnic, regional and religious backgrounds, they have helped reorganize American Christianity. At the heart of the appeal of the television evangelists is a popular religious message created by no one in particular for everyone in general. Although there are exceptions the gospels of the most successful electronic preachers are divorced from any particular tradition. The "health-and-wealth" gospel, for instance, is clearly becoming the most characteristic message in the world of high-rated televised religion.[13] There are many similar earlier gospels presented in books and other literature, but the electronic media are turning the new gospel into the most popular one around. Only the electronic media could do this, for they so easily traverse space and accelerate cultural change, eclipsing or transforming traditional religious faith and practice. To the extent that such electronic expressions of religion eliminate the traditional expressions maintained through print and oral communication, the electronic media could transform the very character of the Christian gospel in American society.

DRAMA AND PERSONA

The most rapidly growing churches in the United States have adopted the basic technological and institutional biases of television: drama and persona. In order to compete for members and contributions, local churches and even entire denominations have established personality-oriented, dramatically structured styles of worship. Some church leaders have introduced into worship the basic principles of drama: character, conflict, plot and setting. Old-style preaching formats are now heavily supplemented on television and in many Protestant churches with various histrionics and musical performances. And in some of the most progressive churches, such as Robert Schuller's Crystal Cathedral and suburban Chicago's Willow Creek Community Church, dramatic productions are a significant part of the congregation's public life, including liturgy.[14] Dramatically speaking these changes are establishing new approaches to church iconography and ritual that resemble the Roman Catholic style more than the historic Protestant style.

Some of the most successful Protestant pastors today have

either a native instinct or a learned ability to create anticipation and build dramatic conflict, thereby engaging their congregations just as television lures its own audiences. Of course such dramatic intrigue is hardly the creation of the television industry. It existed long before the Christian church in rituals of various kinds. Television merely resurrected popular ritual on a national and increasingly an international basis. Even compared with vaudeville and film, which required public theatre attendance, television's technological delivery system is far more potent, delivering drama daily to nearly every household in North America. In the television age people see more drama in one year than previously they saw in a lifetime. Commercial television has created a seemingly insatiable appetite for popular drama, and more than a few churches have decided that if they cannot beat television they are going to join it.

In addition television has accentuated the role of personality in American society. Certainly the human interest in personality transcends the medium of television. Our interest in persona is evident throughout history and most powerfully in the personification of gods. But in the television age persona is among the most important elements of national and international public life. The small television screen effortlessly delivers facial images into the privacy of our domiciles: actors and actresses, news reporters and anchors, talk show and game show hosts, even commercial characters such as one who tries to keep people from squeezing toilet tissue and another who delivers Columbian coffee to town on the back of a mule. Day in and day out no medium matches television's power to build attractive images of people that viewers feel like they know and can even trust.

So far we have tried to paint a picture of the so-called communications revolution as a dynamic interaction between the culture and the various media -- print, oral and electronic. Our goal has been to challenge the overly simplistic notion that one media form will eliminate another. While the electronic media affect cultural life, including religion, they have not eliminated all previous cultures. Instead, the electronic media have shaped American cultural life and altered the mix of available communications channels. Today old and new cultures and media stand side by side, competing for a place in the cacophony of religious and secular voices. Religious faith and practice are a nearly indescribable hodgepodge of images, sounds and words. The electronic media have made it difficult for some traditional expressions of religious faith and practice to survive, but they have hardly eliminated Christianity or other religions. Both as personal faith and as social institution, Christianity is alive and well, although not in precisely the same forms as before humankind discovered how to use the electromagnetic spectrum to communicate with distant places.

In the remaining pages we shall offer some prescriptions for the church, its leaders, its educational institutions and its members. Our goal is largely to allay the typical academic and ecclesiastical fears about the electronic media while staying clear of the technological optimism that characterizes so much popular religious rhetoric. If the mainline churches have bought the dystopian rhetoric about the so-called communications revolution, the evangelicals have bought the utopian version. A reasonable response to the contemporary situation calls for a middle ground that celebrates the new technologies while attempting to use them wisely and discerningly.

A CRAFTED COMBINATION

The church must use a carefully crafted combination of all media forms -- oral, print and electronic. The church should not put all of its media efforts into only one or two media forms. Modern culture exists in and through all three forms simultaneously. Of course some people speak as if the electronic media are the wave of the future, and that other media will become rather insignificant by comparison. But experience in all areas of life shows that oral and print media will continue to play important roles. Writing and printing never completely replaced the spoken word. Similarly, texts might be delivered to readers via video screens instead of paper, but publishing of some kind will survive. Education will always rely upon the "printed" page, although the computer screen might eliminate the need for paper, just as paper itself once replaced parchment.

The difficulty for churches and for religious educators is to determine the best role for each media form in modern culture and in the church. The question "How shall we use the electronic media?" cannot be answered until we first decide what goals these media can accomplish. Each media form has its own potential and its own limitations. Any decision about one medium must be made in the broader context of the mix of available media in contemporary life.

This is by far the most important problem that theological schools will face with regards to the media. The tendency to use the wrong medium for the right problem has led many pastors, churches and denominations into ineffective and sometimes expensive programs. The media are part of the limited resources that can be put to religious uses. Media consume our time, as producers and consumers, and burn away our financial resources. There is no reason to believe that all media are equally good at all tasks. In addition, the problems and opportunities facing religious educators and churches change. Particular media must be matched to specific uses at particular times and places. The interaction of media and culture is too dynamic for anything but careful analysis of each situation. Only the general capacities of individual media are relatively clear and straight-forward.

Oral communication is central to human relationships. All primary groups inevitably depend upon speech as the cement that both creates deep and rewarding relationships and the wrecking ball that can destroy relationships and make life miserable. More than anything else local and community life are contingent upon interpersonal communications, which is the basis for mutual trust and shared views of life. We come to know others primarily through the words we utter and the ones we hear. Such empathic understanding then enables us to serve others. Without this most fundamental of all forms of human communication, we can neither know other peoples' needs nor have any idea how to love and serve them.[15]

> **...the electronic media are the most difficult to assess. Only the fool would claim to know for certain what role they should play in religious faith...**

Congregations and seminaries are similarly dependent upon oral communication. In cases where interpersonal communication is weak, church congregations and seminary classrooms become mere collections of individuals in search of entertainment or information. Interpersonal relationships should be promoted in seminaries and churches just as they should be in offices and homes. This does not mean that families or companies ought not to take the other media seriously, but that orality is crucial to creating the kind of human environment where dialogic communication and truly significant worship and study can take place. Warm, loving congregations attract worshippers, just as personal and caring faculty entice students to seminaries and provide a context for them to learn with their teachers rather than in spite of them.[16]

Moreover, oral communication is crucial to maintaining inter-generational continuity in modern society. The electronic media promote excessive communication within each generation, stratifying society according to rapidly changing life styles. As Margaret Mead suggested decades ago North American culture is the first one where young people learn far more about life from other young people than from older members of society.[17] Teenagers, for example, rightly feel that they have more in common with their peers than with their parents, pastors and teachers. As the electronic media have created new national and international webs of popular culture, they have weakened local, inter-generational communication which was the basis for maintaining traditions over time. If religious faith and practice are to be passed from generation to generation, oral communication will have to be strong within the local body of believers. Videotapes and printed materials can be part of this process of bringing up young people in the faith, but nothing is as powerful and effective as personal, dialogic communication.

Not surprisingly the most successful youth ministries are "relational" rather than formally educational or catechetical. The more church schooling is turned into formal education, the more it is bound to fail in today's world. Young and old people alike feel the need for relationships with people and even with God. Pedantic worship and instructional Sunday School classes often seem irrelevant in this context. But the problem today is most severe among young people who are immersed in the culture of the electronic media. They are easily attracted to ministries that involve them in the consumption of popular culture, such as taking them to Christian rock concerts and other youth events. But such ministries have little or no long-term impact on young people's lives. In fact, such ministries might actually promote intra-generational communication and encourage electronic media consumption, thereby exacerbating the very problems they seek to solve. Churches need to look closely at the very important role that oral communication must play in enhancing communal life and reducing inter-generational discontinuity. Perhaps religious educators could provide leadership in this area.

Strong oral cultures are best able to resist some of the worst aspects of the electronic culture. Most Christians would hardly support the "Christ against culture" attitude of some religious groups. However, many would see the value in some forms of resistance to the transitory national consumer culture that places much of its hope in the endless acquisition of products and the superficial enjoyment to be found in consuming the latest popular art. Such resistance requires strong oral cultures, not just a critical Christian perspective on the broader culture. Oral communication can help keep traditional practices and beliefs alive in the face of competition from the electronic media, while attracting to the church people who are hungry for authentic personal relationships.

Print communication is similarly crucial to the life of the church in the contemporary world. Written texts help enable rational thought, sustained argumentation and systematic reflection. Significant theology would not have been possible without the written word, and it is encumbant upon theological leaders and pastors to help keep the use of this medium alive. The richness and diversity of religious faith and practice today depend upon a literate culture. Indeed, religious and theological traditions now are maintained partly by printed documents, from the tomes of Reformers and the writings of past theologians to canon laws, church orders and even the scriptures themselves.

One task of theological education is to keep religious history alive by retelling it and reinterpreting it for present generations. In today's world we simply are not equipped to do this only through oral communication. Our weak memories and the wide availability of printed materials call for a combination of printed preservation and oral explanation and interpretation. In church and in seminary, in classroom and Sunday School, in office and home, print communication is an irreplaceable link to the past and a crucial mode of current inquiry, discussion and debate. While print can serve other functions, these are highly idiosyncratic to the medium.

Undoubtedly printed materials must be more visually appealing in today's world. We are easily bored visually because of the incessant images of the television and the widespread lure of neon signs and other environmental blights. This is why newspapers are looking more like magazines and why so many magazines have so little text. Compared with books of the nineteenth century today's breed is remarkably colorful and graphic. Only Bibles, academic journals and some reference books have consistently maintained an unadorned visual presence in contemporary culture. The increased "visualization" of print materials certainly has to be examined critically, for the literate content of such materials has been changed as well. But there is no reason to assume that visually appealing materials are necessarily inferior to simply-printed texts. Here, too, the church competes with the broader society.

Because they are relatively new, the **electronic media** are the most difficult to assess. Only the fool would claim to know for certain what role they should play in religious faith and practice. In the early days of radio some religious observers decried the potential power of the medium to eliminate local congregations and usher in "ethereal" churches that would keep people at home on Sunday morning. Others felt that radio preachers would be such skilled speakers that few local pastors would survive the oratorical competition. Through a kind of Darwinian struggle over the airways and across the church pews, good preaching would invariably drive out bad.[18] Sixty years later similar arguments are still made by critics of broadcast religion who believe that radio and television are destroying the fabric of local religious life and established church institutions. But whether any of this is true today is not known for certain. Broadcasting is simply too new a phenomenon for scholars and researchers to have determined the precise effects. The impact of newer electronic media is even more open to interpretation.

Nevertheless, it appears that broadcasting, cable and satellites are more like the spoken word than the printed word. The electronic media are poor vehicles for the kinds of activities that characterize theological and general academic pursuits: scholarship, research, elaborate or extended reasoning and so on. Similarly, the electronic media are not that effective in creating legalistic and bureaucratic cultures. Instead the broadcast media at least seem naturally to gravitate toward narrative and simple exposition. Some critics simplistically criticize radio and television as "mere" entertainment or amusement, thereby suggesting that everything communicated through these media must be artistically and intellectually inferior to the products of other media. This is absurd. Broadcasting's trite and superficial content is largely the product of the commercial institutions that govern most use of the media, not a result of some inherent tendency in the technology. The difference between public and commercial television in the United States makes this abundantly clear.

> **Schools must not only talk about these media... but they must also communicate in and through these media.**

The electronic media's potential for communicating religious perspectives cannot really be known because few religious organizations have had significant funds to experiment with drama, documentaries, docudramas and other narrative forms that can be used effectively on radio and television. Clearly the preaching formats of so many of the televangelists have exposed the limits of the medium as a national pulpit. Audiences for such programs are very small in comparison even to some of the poorest "secular" dramas.[19] Radio is probably a better preaching medium than television because of the centrality of the voice in the broadcast, as the popularity of pre-television preachers such as Harry Emerson Fosdick and Charles Fuller made clear. The electronic media cry out for dramatic productions and for narratives of all kinds.

If the electronic media are to be part of the mix of contemporary religious communication, it is essential that we determine their distinct purpose. Our biggest dilemma is the fact that we might not be able to predict which purposes suit these media. The natural tendency is to assume that every new medium will "replace" an existing one; for example, that videotapes will eliminate the need for Sunday School teachers. Some public school educators made that mistake in the 1970s, when relatively affluent school systems purchased video equipment as a way of relieving teachers of some of their instructional duties. It never worked well. Instead the VCR eventually became merely one more instrument in the labor- intensive and largely dialogic work of instruction. Often new technologies create new uses rather than replacing existing media. The religious community, too, must consider novel uses for the electronic media.

The electronic media are likely the most significant "pre-evangelistic" vehicles ever provided for the church. While radio and television are indeed ineffective at direct evangelism, they are highly important as conduits of cultural change. They strongly shape the underlying values, beliefs and attitudes that permeate American cultural life. From the morality plays of prime-time television to the competitive spirit of televised football and the glorified materialism of commercials, broadcasting shapes American values, which in turn establish the cultural context for American religion. Perhaps the most significant religious use of the electronic media would be to provide alternatives to the values cultivated by Hollywood. The point here is not that everything Hollywood gives us is evil or inferior, but that in the electronic media there are few consistent voices and images of opposition to the secular trends in the mainstream culture.

To put it differently the church has almost no place to stand in American society, where the electronic media largely control the agenda for cultural life. The church needs a space from which to get a hearing, a door into the enormously influential world of popular culture. If the church can figure out how to gain that foothold, both the kinds of communication and the methods of financing them, it might be able to religiously fertilize the culture. The church might also conclude that it should use the electronic media extensively for proclaiming the gospel, but even so the pre-evangelistic function should not be abandoned. People will also seek "entertainment," and the church should not turn over to the rest of the culture the production of such programming.

ASSESSING LIMITS AND POTENTIAL

Religious scholars and educators must address the significance, limits and potential of oral, print and electronic media for religious faith and practice. By now this last point should be abundantly obvious. Religious educators must not get too carried away with the rhetoric about the communications revolution. If they do they might sell their curricula and students down the river of unrealistic hope about the electronic media. Indeed, if religious educators of all types focus their interests and concerns merely on one or two of the major media forms, they will become part of the problem rather than part of the solution. Only if any of these media is inherently demonic or entirely ineffective would churches and seminaries have any reasonable mandate not to address them in the classroom and in research. There is no basis for such an argument. Religious education should look carefully at the implications of the electronic media for instructional goals, curricula and pedagogy. Theological schools have been especially influenced by the academic tone and style of the Reformation. Like its secular counterparts in academe theological education is steeped in the world of the printed and written word. Students and faculty rightly study the same texts and discuss papers on various important but often arcane and esoteric topics. They define, classify and systematize. They build elaborate arguments in favor of significant exegetical questions and concerns. And of course they simply read much about what others have written on relevant topics.

All of this is necessary in theological education, but none of it will lead directly to a greater understanding of the electronic media. The problem is that the electronic and print media communicate differently. As theological students learn to operate effectively in the academic world, they will tend to think and express themselves according to the logic and language of the printed word, not the iconic and dramatic languages of the electronic media. Just as many theologians approach the pulpit as if it were a lecture podium, theological students will mistakenly approach the electronic media as if they were public stages for theological reflection and instruction. They will give us largely ineffective and prosaic videotapes or films cast in pedantic modes and expressed with great logic and system.

Therefore, religious education must be careful not to turn its interest in the electronic media merely into another exercise in academic research. Schools must not only talk **about** these media, however valuable and necessary an exercise that might be, but they must also communicate **in** and **through** these media. Only when a teacher, pastor or theologian is faced with the dilemma of communicating electronically can she or he begin to understand the real problems and potentials of these media. We are not suggesting some type of purely vocational or technical instruction, although theological education is already both. Rather, we are arguing for a curriculum that requires students to consider in a real situation the potential and limits of the electronic media.

Of course it is possible that there is no logical place for the electronic media in curricula or even in the life of the typical seminary. Perhaps the electronic media are not fundamental to educational life, as are the printed and spoken word. But this possibility must not be assumed. Education was not always as literate as it is today. It was once based on oral communication. Moreover, even if religious education itself will not find the electronic media hospitable to its mission and purpose within the seminary walls, such instruction must still educate its students about the function and impact of the electronic media on church and society. This, too, is an important task, although it might not be accomplished without a curriculum that includes media praxis.

No human prophets will be able to predict the ultimate place of the electronic media in the world. At least we can be comforted by the fact that religious faith and practice have survived previous communications revolutions, and that those revolutions were not so revolutionary after all. We know that humans shape history by their actions, including what they do with each new medium that God sends their way. It will be a strong temptation for the church to run wildly with the new media, as some broadcast preachers already have, or to turn the new media over to principalities and powers. The church deserves a voice in the dynamic interplay between the media and the culture, but in the long run only the most visionary religious leaders are likely to claim that voice. Whether or not those visionaries will use the media for the glory of God and in the service of humankind depends in no small measure on the efforts of people in religious education.

JAMES D. NELSON

"We are behind in helping people understand what they see on television, just as we are way behind in helping people understand what they read. The same work needs to be done on the exegesis of a television program as has been done on the exegesis of an historic text or biblical text. Americans tend to see only part of the picture. Somebody else decides what is significant, and we are often inclined to be uncritical. I'd like to see students able to render events at a distance of time and space through a lively historical imagination."

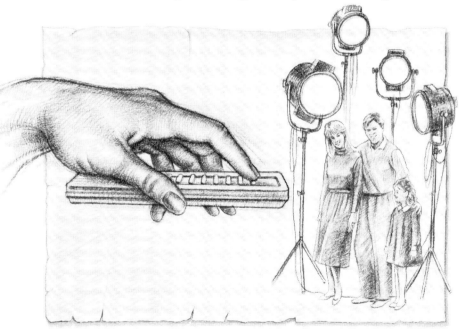

❝ *If I were a producer I would depict visually the lives of ordinary people -- both the religious and non-religious. It's difficult for people to identify with people of the past and to deal with the similarities and differences. One of the things that we lose is the diversity of humanity and the potential of diversity in ourselves. We assume everybody is as we are.* **❞**

41

"The presentation of the China case on television was one of the most powerful events in my experience, especially the presence of those passionate students weeping. As a teacher I was particularly taken by the involvement of their teachers with them -- the gripping image of the teacher going and looking for her students in Tiananmen Square. It reminded me of some of the things that happened in the Vietnam era. We had students who were acting out implications and teachings in radical and honest ways."

"Television produces artifacts and documents which are then useful later on and are irrefutable. It is more difficult to turn time back now, particularly as it is flashed across the world instantly. It is hard to deny that something is happening or has happened. The 1989 China revolution is a case in point, because the old regime attempted to effect the events, and make it as if they had not occurred. We don't know yet how this will work, but my suspicion is that the old regime will not be successful internationally. The degree to which they will be successful nationally we will all be watching."

"In my chapter I am interested in how television is likely to affect the church. I suspect that what television does with relation to the kind of work I do is to furnish me a different way of seeing events than I have ever experienced before. I don't think of this as research unless somebody asks a question about what has happened."

CHAPTER TWO

CRUNCHING THE TRADITION: CHRISTIANITY AND TELEVISION IN HISTORICAL PERSPECTIVE

James D. Nelson

Christianity is a "religion of the book." This classification has become so common that it no longer requires explanation or defense. To assail it either in theory or in practice may prove a tedious if not a precarious enterprise. Yet, if the Christian church is to move with any degree of confidence into the exploitation of electronic media, this commonplace assertion will have to be challenged and examined.

BOOK AND TRADITION

It is our hope here to go behind the appropriation of literature by the church and to challenge the assumption of its essential character with regard to Christianity. It is our contention that "book" is of the *bene esse* rather than of the *esse* of Christianity. There is no intention to assert that the Bible is not necessary to the church, but rather that the necessity of the Bible as literature is historically conditioned and is of a practical rather than a metaphysical character. The transcription and retention of words in literary form is instrumental to the church.

The essential character of Christianity lies in its theological interpretation and existential appropriation of historical events occurring over the several millennia of its continuation. Central among these are the events connected with Jesus of Nazareth in the first century of the common era. But also of relatively great importance is the role of Jesus as messianic culmination of the lengthy historical pilgrimage of Israel and as initiation of a continuing divine-human intercourse in the Christian church. The nature of Christianity is thus constituted by its contention that God's initiative has been in history and that God's intention is reflected in the continuing existence of a people created and preserved by recollection, representation and expansion of God's historical activity.

In line with this thinking we find a primary concern for "tradition." European thought and practice since the Reformation have been very unkind to tradition. Both Renaissance and Reformation contrasted it with and degraded it before literature, particularly ancient literature. The Enlightenment, on the other hand, tended to attack traditional authority and the authority of ancient traditions, whether transcribed or not, in favor of timeless reason and the discovery of new knowledge. The fact is, however, that the survival of historic communities and cultures relies directly upon the establishment, preservation and development of tradition. And the continued existence of Christianity relies on the preservation and extension of Christian tradition through time and space in such a community and by means of continuing cultural adaptations. Thus the success and survival of Christianity as an historical faith requires the preservation and communication of its tradition.

THE FIRST CRUNCHING

In the Apostolic church of the first century, the tradition regarding Jesus and his fulfillment of the messianic expectations of ancient Israel was preserved in the living memories of those who had thus experienced and identified him. These memories and interpretations were communicated directly to others by story and sermon and indirectly by letters and narratives. With the passage of time, and as memories of occurrences came to be replaced by the memories of interpreted events, Gospels and Epistles gained a position of increasing authority in Christian tradition. Literature provided a means for the preservation in stable form of verbal communications of tradition.

The spread of Christianity over the then known world was facilitated by the communication and transportation systems developed and maintained by the great empires and commercial enterprises of the late ancient period. This expansion exerted profound stresses upon the Apostolic traditions as the church severed its close ties with its Semitic cultural rootage and sought expression in largely alien cultures. Particularly threatening to the historically oriented tradition of Christianity and its Hebrew forebear were cultures that disregarded and devalued temporal-historic realities in favor of cosmic and metaphysical constructs. The crystallization and normalization of Christian tradition on the model of a body of approved literary communications (as Bible) were set in motion, hastened and completed by all of these forces.

Before the end of the second century the challenge of passing time, of a changing cultural climate, and of the Gnostic heresy precipitated the regulation of Christian self-identification and communication. The church established at its center a normative body of literary communication (Bible) which was to be regulated in its interpretation by authoritative teachers (bishops) according to conventional formulas (creeds). Here we see the first "crunching of the tradition"[1] as Christianity completed and enthroned the "book" of which it is purported to be "a religion." The historical survival of the Christian community by normative preservation of its tradition marks this response to the engagement of Christianity with the cultural networks of the ancient world.

Yet contrary to conventional Protestant wisdom, scripture and tradition, though certainly distinguishable, can hardly be separated from each other. Christian tradition unrelated with scripture is irregular and abnormal; in short, it must be false tradition. On the other hand, scripture deprived of its standing in and as tradition is disowned and denatured. It is only as tradition that the scriptures have a claim to importance and authority. The Christian scriptures are traditional, and Christian tradition is scriptural. Unwritten tradition is distinct from written tradition, and Bible is distinct from other written tradition, but all are united as tradition.

THE SECOND CRUNCHING

While the challenges presented to the church in the preservation and communication of its tradition in the second century led to a protective circumscription of its common heritage, its response to the opportunity of the fourth century was in a different direction. After almost a century of phenomenal expansion, punctuated by periods of more or less general persecution, Christianity emerged in the fourth century as a religion accepted in and eventually favored by the Roman Empire. Institutions, means of travel, means of communications, social, political and commercial networks that had earlier eased the expansion and development of Christianity now were made available for the specific promotion of its ascendancy over rival religions and institutions.

This status as a favored religion had a constellation of effects on the church. Its connection to a world empire soon demonstrated that its structures for governing its all-important tradition were inadequate to an imperial religion. Scripture, bishop and creed might provide sufficient safeguards for a local tradition but the emergence of the great theological struggles over the trinity and christology in the newly founded Christendom demonstrated their inadequacy for an imperial religion. World Christianity soon gave birth to ecumenical councils, producing ecumenical creeds and a diverse structure of theologian-emperors and ecumenical patriarchs, the former discerned in Byzantine emperors of the East and the latter finally expressed in the Western Papacy.

Meanwhile the dizzy pace of Christian expansion into the cultural sea of world cultures and the influx of great numbers of new Christians with great piles of alien religious and cultural baggage presented Christendom unparalleled promise and threat to its integrity. The phenomenal demographic success of Christianity in the following centuries, particularly in the strongholds of classical and barbaric paganisms, was largely a result of the rapid and thorough assimilation of non-Christian cultural and religious traditional material by the church, both in its imperial and its divergent forms.

As the ecumenical councils were hammering out successive refinements in the formulas governing verbal communications of the tradition, the realms of cultic and social expression of tradition were thrown open in such a way as to permit and promote the appropriation of great quantities of pre-Christian religious and cultural content. While the "crunching of the tradition" in the second century represented a confinement and constriction of the heritage, the "crunching" of the fourth century represented broadening.

This development brought a diversification in practice coupled with a quest for agreement with regard to theological matters controverted among the various local strains of the tradition. Roman imperial Christianity and the medieval Christianity that followed it were marked by major and relatively free developments in the realm of practice coupled with relatively constricted development in thought. The normative structures of creed and canon failed to keep pace with and adequately to govern the developing cultic, social and economic structures of the medieval church.

The social disorder that marked most of Christendom during long periods of this era tended to cripple the church in its ability to keep its tradition in order. Over the millennium ending in the fifteenth century, the connection between the policy and practice, and in certain points the thought of the church, had developed conventions which were in conflict with interpretations of the traditional norms as they were coming to be understood. Intellectual developments like the scholastic theology of the high and late Middle Ages and the Renaissance classicism that continued and reacted against it tended to point out but failed to correct the anomalies that had developed. These factors led to a general cry for reformation of the church in the West from the thirteenth century onward, a demand that led in the sixteenth century to the third "crunching of the tradition" in the Reformation that divided the Western church.

THE THIRD CRUNCHING

The general assumption that dominated the identity of Christianity for the first millennium and one-half of its existence was that the Catholic Church was infallibly faithful to its tradition. It was the belief of Christians in general and an assertion by the teachers and priests of the church that no conflict did or could exist between the tradition as presently and universally practiced and the normative scriptures or even the classic "fathers." In short, an essential, indeed a complete concord was assumed and maintained to exist between the whole of tradition as presently believed and practiced and that of the apostolic church as represented in the scriptures. This position, to be sure, had been challenged, and with increasing regularity during the past three centuries.

The growing scrutiny of ecclesiastical thought and practice as represented in doctrine and canon law by the newly-founded universities had led to organized criticism of longstanding conventions. The crusades had spurred the development of commercial activity and a renewal of urban life, giving birth to major strains in the social system and a search for religious expression appropriate to new states and conditions of life. A new network of travel and communication spread over late medieval Europe, which brought alien ideas and aspirations to light, these often condemned as heretical. The conventions once significantly challenged defended themselves by the force of ecclesiastical and civil law in the Inquisition, but they also sought to defend themselves historically and theologically.

> **Televising well as a requirement to exercise ecclesiastical authority need be no more threatening to the survival of the church than a requirement in sex, age, learning or literary style.**

The upshot was that already in the fourteenth century the Catholic Church as represented by the ecumenical patriarch of the West (the Papacy) was branded by otherwise apparently orthodox Christians as anti-Christian and apostate. With the sixteenth-century Reformers this judgment that the Catholic Church had fallen became the judgment of a significant part of Western Christendom. Thus the tradition and scripture were sundered and contrasted in Reformation thought. The only hope for a faithful Christianity was the more or less general rejection of "tradition" and reconstruction of Christianity on the basis of scripture alone.

The Reformation as a movement "crunching the tradition" represents a systematic and more or less thorough purge of the common tradition brought about by criticism and rejection of accepted structure, thought and practice on the basis of literary standards. The chief Reformers (Luther, Zwingli and Calvin) were young men who were trained in logical argumentation from literary sources by their university educations. Bearers of the social and economic ambitions of their nascent middle-class families, they were educated with hopes for upward mobility and the establishment of parental security. The Renaissance furnished them with the sources and the approach to those sources that placed them in a position to drive home a damning critique of ecclesiastical usage. The universities and early Renaissance figures had established the logical and critical habits of mind and had also brought forth the pivotal literature: first the compendia of biblical and patristic and legal materials from the past, then the writings of the ancients themselves in whole or in part.

In this scene the arrival of Gutenberg was an event of epoch-making significance. The possession and use of authoritative literature in previously inconceivable quantity, quality and affordability significantly altered the authority structures of Western Christendom at the beginning of the sixteenth century. Transformed patterns of communication had brought the literature to light and afforded new approaches in its interpretation and application. The new device flooded the marketplace with previously unavailable means for reform.

The impact of the appearance of the scriptures in Greek and Hebrew, thus going behind the whole Latin Vulgate presupposition of Western medieval theology, is difficult to overestimate. Armed with dialectic method and equipped with the critical method and already developed demolition work of the Renaissance humanists, the Reformers set out to purge Christian tradition of the accretions of more than a millennium of history. The mandate given by the second "crunching" in the fourth century for the assimilation of massive quantities of pre-Christian gentile thought and practice was rescinded.

Modern Christendom was born as the presses poured forth the old sources and the new products of Reformation thinkers and ecclesiastics. Appeal was thus made to the judgment and commitment of an explosively expanding audience. As never before the tools and materials of tradition and its regulation were made available to ordinary people. The fullest appropriation of the capacity of the press to provide access to the tradition to all classes of Christians did not take place until the religious waves of Puritanism and Pietism were felt in European Protestantism.

These movements produced a truly literate mass culture for the first time and thus opened the door to a nearly endless proliferation of narrowly normative Christianities, that is, the sects and denominations of modern Christendom. Flowing forth from these same movements were appropriations of other emerging techniques and technologies for the propagation of religious thought, commitment and activity.

A religious journalism grew up side by side with secular endeavors of the same sort. Massive religious convocations of persons for religious communication and exercise became a feature of Christianity in all sectors of the modern West as mass cultures were facilitated by modern commerce, politics and transportation. These conjoined with popular religious awakenings from the eighteenth century onward to produce the systems of revivalism. After a long period of apparent indifference toward non-Western peoples, Protestantism took up missionary activity along the lines of its commercial and political interest beginning in the eighteenth century and with previously unparalleled zeal in following centuries.

Pietism, revivalism and the missionary movement all reflected an interest in transcending the particularity and sectarian narrowness that flowed out of the third "crunching" of the tradition at the Reformation. Though they have not shown strong signs of any formal withdrawal from the Protestant rejection of "tradition" other than the normative tradition of the Bible, such groups have shown their willingness to cooperate across sectarian and denominational lines to communicate a common message and carry forward humanitarian work. The development and exploitation of forms of mass communications other than publication and the public press have demonstrated their ability to move the church once more toward a more ecumenical and secularly involved relation to its tradition and its communication.

A FOURTH CRUNCHING?

The technical developments of the present century in the field of communications have opened the doors to the distribution of the church's tradition to all levels of society as well as to and in every human culture. The limitation of such long-range communications to verbal and literary means alone has also been breached, making possible the development of charismatic authority figures of undreamed of power and influence.

These possibilities are particularly nascent in the medium of television. Although it is certainly too early to predict the influence this medium will have, its potential opens the door to the possibility of yet a fourth "crunching of the tradition," one in which the closedness and the narrowing of the third may be transcended as Christendom finds a new and common vision and voice.

HIERARCH, THEOLOGIAN AND PROPHET

Among other historical variables, arrangements with regard to authority roles seem to be particularly sensitive to the character and function of communications media and technologies employed in a particular society. It should therefore prove enlightening to make a cursory survey of the historic performance of Christianity in that regard. Our focus will be upon the relative empowerment and ascendancy of various types of authority figures in their correlation with emerging and developing media and technologies of communication.

For the sake of this scrutiny of historic Christianity we single out three authority roles: that of hierarch, that of theologian and that of prophet.[2] The former two are grounded on custom or on law, while the third is, properly speaking, a "charismatic" role in which one is installed as a result of personal conviction of authority and its communication to others. At the outset of Christian history these roles are not clearly differentiated and at no point are they mutually exclusive. But as the Christians increased in number and in geographical and cultural diffusion, the organization of the church became more definite and complex. Early second-century bishops, like Ignatius of Antioch or Polycarp of Smyrna, readily combined the role of hierarch with that of prophet and perhaps also that of theologian, but with the passage of time the differentiation tended to become more hard and fast.

There is more by far to be gained than lost in crunching the tradition for television.

In fourth-century Egypt it is instructive to look at Athanasius, Arius and Anthony. Athanasius, as no other in his time, combined all three roles. He was a metropolitan bishop of immense though unstable power. He functioned as a highly influential theological figure, both orally and literarily. Finally he was able to stir strong popular support and authority as a persecuted witness for "truth."

Arius was also able to combine the three roles but in different degrees. Although he was a priest and early on utilized hierarchal status in promoting his convictions, he developed in the midst of the controversy over his views into a major and apparently carefully crafted charismatic figure. The party that gathered around him promoted his theological views and his personal popularity by what was in effect an ancient media blitz, including placards, slogans and jingles as well as more serious literary efforts at theological explication.

Our third Egyptian, Anthony, was a "prophet" or charismatic role figure pure and simple. In fact, his person as presented in promotional literature by none other than Athanasius himself became a role model for the whole class of charismatic figures and movements associated with asceticism and monasticism. Anthony as the classic "desert father" was a creation of Athanasius' pen and was to become a paradigmatic authority figure of immense influence in the Christianity of the next millennium, both in East and West.

AUTHORITY ROLES AND COMMUNICATION MEDIA

With these three roles and figures in mind we will look at the function of means of communication as these means relate to their establishment and exercise.

The role of such means in the creation of a hierarch is more formal than dynamic. To be sure, the traditions that validate customary roles are preserved and disseminated by means of communication, but here the emphasis is more on stability and structure. The same could be said for the formal legal mandates for such roles. On the other hand, a hierarch must depend on communications for the exercise of authority and upon preserved communications for knowledge of the precedents upon which opinions and decisions are generally based. Thus media are more important to the exercise than to the establishment of the authority of a hierarch.

A theologian, on the other hand, unless also established in authority as an "official" theologian and thus effectively as a hierarch (like a university professor or a doctor of the church) will be established in a position of authority by convincing others that he or she is indeed worthy of credit. This is generally done by relating one's ideas to communications of belief and to thought already regarded as credible and orthodox and by means of communicated argument establishing the credibility of one's own position. Thus new communications are a basis for both the establishment and the exercise of authority by a person in the theological role.

The establishment of a person as a prophet or charismatic figure is still more completely reliant on the effective application of more or less public communications. To be sure conventions and sometimes even legislation do emerge with regard to validation of such figures, but the status and authority of "prophets," or saints, or martyrs, or monks or whatever such persons are being called relies upon their own communications, or communications about them, which lead people to credit them with authority and to follow their leadership in thought and practice. In view of this analysis it should be fairly obvious why the third authority role will provide the focus for our further treatment.

Clearly the most popular subject of Christian communications through the centuries has been the creation and application of authority roles which must be identified with our third class, the prophet or "charismatic." The only others that even come close in overall published verbiage are the disputations of the theologians.

It is instructive to review the emergence and promotion of classic models of this "charismatic" type through the centuries. The charismatic model that clearly dominated the ancient church was that of the confessor/martyr. This model was the product and producer of a whole body of idiosyncratic literature and of a popular cultus involving contemplation and veneration of their deeds, their bodily remains and ultimately of their likenesses in art and action. The whole development related with the "saints" appears to be a more or less direct outgrowth of this particular model.

A second type of charismatic emerging in the ancient church and dominant in Christendom from the fourth through the fifteenth centuries is that built around Anthony, that of the ascetic/monastic role. This model was developed and exercised in much the same manner as was that of the confessor/martyr, but like the confessor, and unlike the martyr, such "prophets" were in a position to exercise authority actively and not merely to serve as an image to be manipulated by others. These athletic Christians of the desert and the monastery continued the development of the saintly model as a dominant factor in the life and practice of Christendom down to the Protestant Reformation.

The sixteenth-century Reformation brought to full expression a third "prophet" or charismatic role, that of the proclaimer/evangelist. Although by no means entirely new this model did not come into its own as a type of charismatic authority until the modern era. It was in the persona of the Reformers themselves and ideally in their concept of the evangelical preacher that the model reached clear expression. In significant ways the model is still in the process of formation.

The modern church is giving form to yet another charismatic type which we may call the servant/humanitarian. Unlike the confessor/martyr who is moving against the world and the ascetic/monastic who is moving away from the world, and like the proclaimer/evangelist who is moving toward the world, the servant/humanitarian finds expression within and ideally as the world. This new class of secular saint, classically exemplified by figures like Albert Schweitzer and Mother Teresa, is profoundly lay-identified despite technical status to the contrary. A figure like John R. Mott comes to mind in this regard. He can best be seen as a transitional figure between the proclaimer/evangelist and the servant/humanitarian models.

Having set forth these four types of prophet or charismatic it remains to relate them and our three authority roles to a carefully selected and provocative set of historic personalities.

PROPHETIC OR CHARISMATIC AUTHORITY AND MASS MEDIA

As one reviews church history with a view to bringing media personalities to light, a handful of figures may be singled out. For our present enterprise we will analyze and classify: Bernard of Clairvoux

(1090?-1153), Francis of Assisi (1182?-1226), Martin Luther (1483-1546), John Wesley (1703-1791), Billy Graham and Albert Schweitzer.[3] In each one of these cases we have to do with a person who gained immense popular attention and drew upon himself the loyal allegiance of a great number of people.

Although Bernard idealized martyrdom he gave his life to the fulfillment of the ascetic/monastic model. While he exercised a preaching and promoting function, its real goal was recruitment for the ascetic/mystical approach to God. Holder of no ecclesiastical office other than as head of the monastery of Clairvoux, Bernard was the most renowned and truly powerful figure of his age. He was no Pope, but was in fact able to "make" and "direct" pontiffs. A person of reputedly irresistible magnetism he was an extremely effective charismatic figure. In his public development and function we find Bernard exploiting the system of movement and communications developing around and out of the crusading movement in the promotion of which he played such an important role. His power and influence would be largely inconceivable apart from that growing network.

Francis of Assisi idealized and sought to promote the ascetic/monastic model both in himself and in others. He, however, moved more actively into the proclaiming/evangelistic function. Arising as the Franciscans did in the developing commercial towns of Italy, we find the impulse of their founder toward, rather than away from, the world. They sought to actualize both evangelical proclamation and humanitarian service while maintaining a primary focus on ascetic identity. Although we lack a significant body of writings from Francis' hand (unlike Bernard he was not a literary person), the lore that developed around his personality and its contemporary and subsequent influence are unparalleled in Christian history. Even a cursory glance at the concerns and responses of the persons surrounding him reveals that the man became virtually a living icon in his own time, thus a media personality in the modern sense.

Martin Luther, unlike the other figures, had a primary claim to official status as an official theologian and thus in our sense was a hierarch. He also credentialed himself and functioned in the theological role, engaging in the disputive dialogue of the theologians. His most distinctive role, and the one that validates his place in church history, is his status and function as a proclaiming/evangelistic charismatic figure. A clear sign of such status in literary cultures is the preservation of massive bodies of assorted literary materials. Luther, as the first such person to utilize the services of printed literature, is the beneficiary and victim of his contemporary fame and reputation. His person and style created difficulties for those who would virtually canonize him in his own time as they had Francis and

Bernard. But despite his "warts" he managed to accumulate about his person a degree of reverence and authority unmatched in his age. His personality may have managed to prevent his beatification in his lifetime, but the speed with which he was so treated after his death is indicative of the forces at work in his popular reputation and cultural authority.

Although John Wesley claimed an official sanction for his work on the basis of his fellowship at Lincoln College, Oxford, and engaged the theological community in vindication of his doctrinal tenants, his main concern was not with the theological guild but with the common people. Thus his authority was neither hierarchal nor theological in the senses we have proposed. Wesley's was a charismatic authority of the proclaimer/evangelist type. He emerged on the public scene in his late thirties as a controversial, often publicly reviled personality. He gained personal authority as a spiritual director and evangelical preacher with a well organized and highly disciplined circle of adherents. He promoted his reputation through public preaching and organization of those affected by that preaching. He further recruited and directed a cadre of "assistants" who acted as extensions of his personal authority with his expanding body of followers.

An important part of this developing pattern was the publication of literature for popular consumption. Wesley was a consummate religious publisher and journalist. An unusually large part of his literature was given over to vindication of his personal activity and authority, particularly in the form of his published *Journals*. Scrutiny of the massive bulk of Wesley's preserved writings and editions demonstrates the character of his authority and the role that his use of techniques for communication played in its emergence and exercise. As with Luther before him a large portion of these writings is sermonic in character and evangelistic in intent.

In coming to Billy (William Franklin) Graham we have intentionally passed over such luminous candidates from the development of the proclaimer/evangelist in modern revivalism as George Whitefield and Charles Grandison Finney. Graham emerges as a person of outstanding reputation and authority in the United States during the post-World War II period. He has developed a substantial organization to promote and publicize his work as an evangelist and has used to good effect ecclesiastical networks and media of journalism and the production of devotional, edifying and sermonic literature.

Graham is of particular interest in this discussion, however, because he has moved into mass communications in a way that may prove epoch-making. By means of electronic amplification and modern theatrical lighting effects, he has managed to bend the huge and numerous public athletic facilities that have become an international phenomenon to his use as a proclaimer/evangelist. From a platform of massive gatherings in sports arenas and stadiums, Graham has managed to move to the incomparably larger audiences of network television. The result has been the attainment of unparalleled celebrity and religious authority around this personality. Although Graham has been very guarded in his exercise of the authority he has thus attained, there is ample evidence of his impact on Christianity and American culture in the several decades of his ascendancy.

Choice of Dr. Albert Schweitzer to represent prophetic/charismatic authorities of the servant/humanitarian model is an intentional effort to see this type at the height of its development. This sort of "secular saint" has been appearing in increasing numbers since the late Middle Ages. The practical impulses of

"Video may liberate ignored and unrealized dimensions of ancient narratives as they are bent to that medium."

Puritanism, Pietism and evangelicalism in seventeenth and eighteenth-century Protestantism gave it a strong stamp of lay identity and support. Beside the inward interest of those historic movements there emerged a strong and widely disseminated impulse to humanitarian service. Beside the evangelistic and devotional concerns of a Philipp Spener stood the humanitarian enterprises of an August Francke. Beside the preaching and organizing of the Wesleys also stood the social reformation concerns of the so-called Clapham Sect. A similar correlation can be shown with relation to major proclaimer/evangelist figures in American revivalism.

Although Schweitzer's threefold career as theologian, musicologist and physician might be expected to confuse us as to who or what he actually was, its real effect was simply to accentuate his authentic identity. In the abandonment of brilliant careers as a theological scholar and as a musical scholar and virtuoso, Schweitzer emerges as a confessor/martyr. As he embraces his least promising career as a physician and carries out its practice in Africa, he appears as a dramatic sort of ascetic/monastic. In his proposed "wordless" human service in reverence for life, the renowned theologian was a proclaimer/evangelist of monumental scope. All of these historic roles were brought to focus in his exemplification of the service/humanitarian model. The symbiotic activity of Schweitzer and mass media was a public phenomenon of immense impact and abiding influence. Journalists of all kinds never relented in their preoccupation with Schweitzer and were successful in creating a world personality of unusual reputation and power. Although Schweitzer is now absent from the scene, his personal authority has managed to survive the attacks of numerous well publicized debunkers. Such attacks have generally proven more damaging on those who make them than upon Schweitzer's public reputation, regardless of objectively verifiable authenticity.

AUTHORITY FIGURES AND TELEVISION

The interplay of prophet or charismatic Christian authority figures and mass communications shows no signs of coming to an end. Each emerging technical refinement has apparently raised the stakes and escalated the impact. That hierarchs and theologians should be apprehensive about such developments should come as no surprise. There can be little doubt that new techniques threaten the dominance these two authority roles have had in the Church and over its tradition.

There is, however, no reason to assume that they need pose any unusual threat to the substance or structures of the tradition or of the church itself. "Televising well" and being able to project an engaging and magnetic personal image as a requirement to exercise ecclesiastical authority need be no more threatening to the survival of the church and its tradition than a requirement in sex, age, learning or literary style. The tradition has managed to survive earlier media "crunchings." There is no reason to assume that our present discomfort need signal unusual or unexampled danger for Christianity.

Indeed, there may yet be grounds to resurrect the sanguine expectations with which television was greeted on its emergence on the popular scene four decades ago. Even hierarchs and theologians may yet congratulate themselves on its advent and exercise. The effective utilization of a new wrinkle in communications technology has never been immediate or without effort, pain and patience. "Hardware" is generally years ahead of the "software" that would render it maximally useful. It remains for the Christians and their tradition to risk the price of faithful communication in the new media. There is more by far to be gained than lost in "crunching the tradition" for television.

Unfortunately, petulance is rife among Christian authority figures in the face of yet another "crunch." Change of any kind is threatening to those who assume they have arrived. Such concerns for security of status lead us to ignore important and basic continuity between the old and the new communications. Ecclesiastical journalists were quick to recognize the possibilities offered by experiments carried out by their secular counterparts in television. The possibilities and peculiarities of television as a medium for drama are just now beginning to be realistically perceived and responded to. Christian use of it is still somewhere in "kindergarten." Students of the scriptures have begun to discern the possibility that video may liberate ignored and unrealized dimensions of ancient narratives as they are bent to that medium. The rightful impact of television with its dispersion of learners and immediacy of approach on our school and book-bound educational systems is still "light years" from perception, to say nothing of realization.

But we may be on the verge of entering the "stone age" of video education with our most advanced experiments. In terms of televising such a complex and personal event as a worship service or even a sermon, current comprehensions and techniques are about as far from a satisfactory production as televised baseball was in 1950. If worship were equally simple and received anything like the same exposure and experimentation as the national pastime, we might expect an equally suitable product after a few decades of experience. So much for cautious optimism for a televised tradition.

What about the really weighty stuff like theology? For centuries the disquisitions of theologians have been greeted with little popular enthusiasm when delivered by whatever medium. The function of literature in their enterprise has been practically definitive of its essence. Can there be any hope that some course may be found between "dry as dust" and "bland as pablum" for the practitioners of the church's intellectual enterprise? Although abandonment of literary media is far from indicated in the present or even foreseeable situation, there do seem to be reasons for hopeful thoughts about televised theology.

The present author wishes to propose that, contrary to popular opinion, literature is a secondary medium for critical reflection like theology. Behind the critical mental sciences is a long history of cultivation and function in the oral exercise of living dispute. At first it seemed that this assertion would only go as deep as the councils of the church and the rise of medieval universities, focused as they were on the exercise of disputation. But the mark of verbal debate is far more deeply stamped on philosophy, theology, government and jurisprudence than such shallow rootage would imply. The present writer is convinced that critical thought was formed and nurtured in the fires of conflicting perceptions and judgments in untold and long forgotten tribal councils and tribunals. What we actually possess in the most polished treatises of theologians from modern universities are thinly veiled refutations and counter proposals to unseen debaters past and present. But where does debate get us on television?

The most celebrated media events identified with debate, the so-called presidential debates, promise little, if anything, relative to critical thought. After dismissal of this horrible example, one may still think of "great debates" from history as produced by Steve Allen. They do offer something in regard to the historical character and function of ideas. An experiment in video debate in a more formal sense has been made by William Buckley on public television. Despite its rather rigid technical format and the somewhat peevish demeanor of the resident debater, it has enjoyed unusual popularity for a program marked by such rigorous intellectual enterprise.

The fact is, however, that completely apart from these examples of televised disputation there is a major enterprise of the medium that has come more and more to assume that form and role. Reference is to a great preponderance of so-called news broadcasting. Although the presentation of "news" on television began its career in the narrative style of the public press and the radio, the immediacy of the medium and public interest in televised conflict has led broadcast news into the induction of disputation between absent but often recorded and depicted adversaries, intellectual or otherwise. The fact is that presidential debates have emerged as an opportunity for viewers to determine whether the nightly disputation *in absentia* is genuine and perhaps more importantly, whether the actual disputants are capable of sustaining the real face to face combat. No claim can here be made that the nightly news has shown the way for theological television; rather the essential function of theology as disputation and the capacity of television to sustain that debate are a combination of genuine promise for the future of a lively theological tradition on video. Even theology may not be "crunched" beyond repair by television.

The dizzy pace of recent progress in communications technology coupled with some unsatisfactory experience has left many Christian leaders fearful and angry. Television, in particular, greeted four decades ago with utopian expectations has become for many the enemy at home. There can be no doubt that adaptation to this medium will exact a price of the Christian tradition, but only as that price is accepted and the church loosens its grip on familiar and comfortable accommodations of the past can the promise of this new medium be realized. The crunching of the tradition necessarily involves a useful mutilation of its message as it is subjected to and transmitted by this much seen but little understood medium. The tradition must once more be surrendered to be shared anew.

THOMAS E. BOOMERSHINE

"I almost never use my trained critical faculties, as you call them, when I watch television. I am a sucker for involvement. I am almost instantly sucked in, and I suspend virtually all critical faculties until later. The whole notion of Television Awareness Training has always struck me as absurd. I can do it, but television has a degree of power to involve me that is awesome. I have to be careful, because I can be really taken in."

"*If I had all the money in the world and could produce any program I wanted, it would be an audiovisual translation of the Bible. It would be, for our time, another Latin Vulgate or Luther's German translation.* **"**

"I watch a lot of television. It depends on how much I watch whether I feel guilty. I generally watch sporting events. I graze mercilessly. That is what I do when I really want to escape."

"In terms of television and my work as a biblical scholar, I am increasingly aware that I look for, especially late at night, someone to pray with, someone to think about God with. I look but I don't find. I know I am not the only one who is searching for some late-night electronic way to be related to God. I suspect there are lots and lots of people like me, using television at all hours of the day and night to try to cope with their lives, looking for God."

"My picture of television is as an electronic camera. It is the reason why story is the most natural form for television. That is why I am optimistic about television. Story is the most natural form for the children of Israel throughout the ages. One of the ironies about the present for me is that this is not being experienced or even recognized. I feel as if I am a person before my time."

"My work on storytelling, and on the degree to which even when it was written down it was experienced as oral, has convinced me in my deepest mind and soul that television is not a threat. Indeed, the whole Christian community was formed in relation to a medium and a culture other than that of writing. I am not afraid of the electronic media in a way that I think most people are. They seem to be, at some foundational level, so spooked that they have to attack the electronic media in order to defend their tradition."

"God has given us electronic communications and the possibility of forming a worldwide communications community in order to save us from ourselves. The church has a primary mission as a part of the plan of God to be an agent for the salvation of the world at the time when we have the technology to destroy it. I do not see any religion that has the same power for peace and reconciliation as is present in the gospel of Jesus Christ."

CHAPTER THREE

A NEW PARADIGM FOR INTERPRETING THE BIBLE ON TELEVISION

Thomas E. Boomershine

In the history of Western Christianity there is a discernible correlation between major changes in communications technology, schisms in the communities of the Judeo-Christian tradition, and the development of new paradigms of biblical interpretation.[1] In each period of adjustment to the culture generated by a new dominant communications medium and a new paradigm of biblical interpretation, there is a pattern of response that can be characterized as resistance, appropriation and capitulation.

MODES OF INTERPRETATION
AND COMMUNICATIONS MEDIA

The conservative response in each age is to resist the new culture generated by the new medium while incorporating the medium into the old culture and its hermeneutics, or its methods of interpretation. Thus, in the period of the adaptation of the tradition of Israel to the manuscript paradigm, Pharisaic Judaism resisted the Hellenistic culture associated with writing. It incorporated writing and the written law into Jewish culture and even formed a canon of the written law. But the written law was studied and appropriated in the context of the oral law and the characteristic cultural patterns of the oral age. The ongoing formation of the oral law first in the Mishnah and then the Talmud continued the primary oral hermeneutic of biblical interpretation. Interpreters of the tradition continued to be authorized by the oral processes of rabbinic education rather than in any sense by publication of written works.

Christian Judaism appropriated the new medium and its culture and formed a new synthesis which integrated the old medium and its culture into a new hermeneutical paradigm. The struggle between the Antiochene and Alexandrian schools of literal and allegorical interpretation were the primary sign of the tensions in this new paradigm. The Antiochene wing maintained close relationships with Rabbinic Judaism while the world of Hellenistic philosophy formed the primary cultural matrix of the Alexandrians. In the end the new synthesis formed by Christianity adopted the allegorical methods of Hellenistic culture while maintaining essential continuity with the more literal methods of interpretation generated by the

61

oral culture which gave birth to the scriptures. To state this thesis/ antithesis/synthesis in terms of persons, the tension between Origen and Jerome resulted in Augustine's new hermeneutical synthesis.

Gnosticism in both its Jewish and Christian forms can be seen as a capitulation response in which the new medium and its culture became so dominant that the old medium and its culture were rejected. The highly individualistic culture of the world of writing with its consuming interest in speculative and creative ideas became the norm of biblical interpretation. The new culture and its values generated a hermeneutical system and institutions that actively sought to dissociate the sophisticated literary philosophical present from the primitive oral narrative past.

In the period of adjustment to the paradigm of print and the culture with which it was associated, the Roman Catholic response was to resist the new culture of which the printing, distribution and historical interpretation of the scriptures were a part. In the aftermath of the Council of Trent, Catholics appropriated the essential patterns of the culture associated with printing. But in relation to biblical interpretation, this adaptation maintained strict subordination to the cultural patterns and "fourfold" hermeneutical paradigms of the manuscript period. In no way was independent interpretation of the scriptures allowed to compromise the tradition.

Protestantism adopted the new medium and its culture and developed a new synthesis that maintained essential continuity with the tradition. Luther and Calvin were biblical scholars who generated a massive series of printed texts, including vernacular translations, commentaries on the original Greek and Hebrew texts, and doctrinal systems that used the original texts as the primary source. The hermeneutical system was the development of theological doctrine based on a literal interpretation of the biblical texts. This new hermeneutic made possible the widespread distribution of the texts and the formation of communities of independent biblical interpreters that were held together by a common hermeneutical framework.[2]

Protestant scholasticism capitulated to the culture of the university and rejected both the old culture and the old medium. The university rather than the church became the primary institutional matrix for this form of culture Christianity.

Finally, in the age of silent print, in various stages throughout Europe and America, the historical critical study of the Bible as a document to be read in silence was resisted by Catholics, Protestant supernaturalists and fundamentalists, as well as orthodox Jews.[3] In each instance the new medium and the study of the Bible as an historical document has gradually been incorporated into the old culture. But the synthesis of a scientific interpretation of the Bible and the culture of the Enlightenment first took place within the mainstream of the Protestant churches. The Protestant churches appropriated the new medium and its culture and created a new hermeneutical paradigm while maintaining continuity with the tradition. The scientific societies for the study of the Bible, such as the Society of Biblical Literature and the Society for New Testament Studies, are the institutional offspring of this paradigm shift. The radical liberal tradition capitulated to the culture of the university and eliminated the basic characteristics of the old medium, for example, the memorization and recital of the scripture.

Thus, the major changes in the dominant communications medium of Western culture are closely correlated with the megatrends of biblical interpretation. This in turn sheds light on the sources of reformation and schism in the history of Western Christian communities. There is a close correlation between the ecclesiastical divisions in the history of Western Christianity, paradigm shifts in biblical interpretation, and changes in the systems of communication.

CURRENT BIBLICAL SCHOLARSHIP
IN THE LIGHT OF MEDIA HISTORY

The implications of this theory for the present context of biblical interpretation are arresting. In relation to communications technology the twentieth century has witnessed the most extensive changes in the media of communication since the development of writing. The printing press was only a more efficient and uniform way of producing written materials while silent reading was a change in the way in which writing was normally perceived. But the elements of continuity between the printed book and the written manuscript were extensive. Books like manuscripts were ink marks on paper pages that were bound together in books and read with the eyes. Both were distributed by being moved from place to place and required extensive training in order to be perceived.

Electronic communications technology is a radically different medium of communication. Television, for example, employs no paper, has widely varied distribution systems, and is perceived by both eyes and ears. It is instantly available and requires no special education in order to be perceived. The only medium change that compares in magnitude with the shift from written to electronic communications is the shift from orality to literacy. In light of the changes in biblical interpretation that took place in response to earlier media shifts, we live at a critical juncture in the history of biblical interpretation.

The church's response to this new medium and its culture has not generated a new paradigm for the transmission and interpretation of the Bible. The most powerful interpreters of the Bible on television are conservative evangelicals and Pentecostals, most of whom have little or no scholarly training. The Bible is talked about constantly but is rarely presented for its own sake. The interpretation of the Bible in the present world of electronic media is a capitulation to American media culture and is profoundly flawed in ways that do not maintain essential continuity with the tradition. The new culture that has developed along with television has become the norm for biblical interpretation. What will sell on American television has become the primary norm of exegetical validity.

To the minimal degree that the Bible itself is presented, the paradigm of biblical interpretation is the conservative wing of biblical interpretation that was developed as a part of the Enlightenment and post-Enlightenment periods. The Bible is literally waved in front of the eyes as a reference source to support a wide range of theological, historical and political positions.

❝❝ Biblical scholarship continues to live and work in the medium world of silent print as if nothing has changed since the late nineteenth century. ❞❞

But any notion of either encouraging independent study of the Bible or of the ambiguity of its witness is foreign to this use of the Bible as the support for American conservative culture.

The community of biblical scholarship and the churches which it serves have almost exclusively resisted electronic media and its culture. The guild has refused to enter into the interpretation of the Bible in the culture of electronic media. Apart from a few isolated and poorly funded videos, there are virtually no television programs on the Bible produced by the major Protestant and Catholic churches and their scholarly leaders. Computers, which make possible the electronic processing of texts, have been enthusiastically integrated into the paradigm of historical critical scholarship. But the world of audio tapes and records, television and films has been an alien culture for orthodox biblical interpretation. At this point in history the best biblical interpreters of our culture have abandoned the defense and commendation of responsible interpretation of the biblical tradition in the most powerful communications medium of our age. That task has been given over to self-appointed religious entrepreneurs. In the age of the greatest media change since the development of writing, biblical scholarship continues to live and work in the medium world of silent print as if nothing has changed since the late nineteenth century.

A projection on the basis of the trends of the past would suggest that this response will become increasingly retrogressive and will result in a withdrawal of the interpretive community from the dominant culture into a defensive posture. This response is not necessarily cataclysmic. Those parts of the tradition that have resisted earlier media changes, such as Rabbinic Judaism, Roman Catholicism, and conservative/fundamentalist Protestantism, maintained their communities by making relatively minor adjustments in the previous systems of biblical interpretation. But the culture that is being formed by electronic media and the people who are a part of that culture will thereby be ignored. The consequences of allowing this travesty of authentic biblical interpretation to go unchallenged in the present religious and political context will be great.

However, while biblical scholarship has not consciously addressed the issue of media change, the theory does explain the fracturing of the historical critical consensus that has taken place in the last two decades. Rather than being the progressive vanguard of the future, historical criticism is increasingly in a position of defending and preserving an earlier culture that is threatened by present developments. The collapse of biblical theology as a strong and viable hermeneutic, the emergence of narrative theology and literary critical methods of exegesis, the impact of semiotics and deconstruction, the development of social science methods of analysis: all are connected by a common epistemological thread which moves away from the distinction between the phenomenal and the noumenal to the phenomena of sense experience itself. In electronic media and its cultures, what is known is what is seen and heard. The theory would suggest that the declining impact of historical critical scholarship and the collapse of its scientific framework is a symptom of a change in the culture. These developments in biblical scholarship are responses to that new culture and its ways of knowing. This effort is more likely to succeed, however, if the need for a new paradigm of biblical interpretation is addressed directly.

A PARADIGM FOR BIBLICAL INTERPRETATION IN ELECTRONIC MEDIA

The theory stated as simply as possible is as follows. The transmission and interpretation of the Bible is a process of communication. The meaning of communication events is directly influenced by the means or media of communication in any particular cultural setting. This fact is particularly evident when new communications technologies emerge and gradually establish a new communications system. The meaning of the old system of interpretation changes and becomes associated with the past rather than the present. The old system can only be maintained by cutting the connection to the emerging new culture, generally by attacking the new medium and the culture with which it is associated. Inevitably, however, even the maintenance of the old system requires adjustments to the new communications situation and the old hermeneutic is modified.[4]

The transmission and interpretation of the Bible in a new communications system and its various cultural matrices require the development of a new paradigm. Some of the elements in the paradigms of biblical interpretation are: the formation of the biblical traditions themselves for transmission in the new medium, the development of systems of production and distribution, the formation of a hermeneutic that will make possible meaningful connections between the traditions in the new medium and the original tradition, and a process for the training and accreditation of interpreters.

Furthermore, with the addition of each new paradigm of biblical interpretation for a new medium and its culture, the previous paradigms are not discarded but are integrated into the new paradigm. Thus, a new paradigm is defined by: 1) the medium in which the Bible itself is transmitted and experienced, 2) the media mix in which the Bible is interpreted, 3) the system of production and distribution by which both the Bible and its interpretation is made available, and 4) the hermeneutic or interpretive framework by means of which the biblical traditions are connected with the present.

TRANSMEDIAZATION: THE BIBLE IN ELECTRONIC MEDIA

The first step is to put the biblical tradition into the new medium, a "transmediazation of the texts." In each new media age this is the first task. Thus, the transition to manuscript technology required that the oral traditions be edited so that they could be written down in manuscripts. In the era of print new critical texts and vernacular translations were developed for the production of printed Bibles. And the silent print era has been associated with the multiplication of a wide range of study Bibles that are designed to be used in silent study.

In each case the central traditions about God were put into the new medium of the age in a loving and responsible manner that preserved continuity with the traditions of the past. Through this process the Bible has been made available to the new culture that was formed in association with each new communications technology. Furthermore, these new texts and translations have been resisted by those who were opposed to any form of cultural accommodation. What is needed, therefore, is an electronic Bible that accomplishes the same purpose for the culture of the electronic age.

The transmediazation of the Bible into television will require that the biblical tradition be presented as sounds and images on a screen rather than as printed marks on a page. The production of a Bible that is composed of sounds and images rather than written texts, however, requires a different process, both in the study of the original manuscripts and in the production of an audio-video translation. A whole new set of factors influence the meaning of the text when it is presented in sounds and images. Rhythm, intonation, attitude, volume, repetition of sounds and emotion are major factors in oral recitation in ways that are largely irrelevant for a written translation. And the images of the text have not really been considered at all as a part of biblical translation. Thus, our present methods for the study of the texts of the Bible do not produce information about the sounds and images of the text.

The first step in the development of a Bible for television will be to gain an understanding of the sounds and images of the biblical texts in their original languages and cultural contexts. How did the Bible originally sound? What were the images that were called forth by the texts? The exegesis of the texts as sound and image will require two interactive stages of investigation. The aural and visual signs of the texts will need to be understood against the background of the sounds and images of the cultures of the ancient world.

The sociology and psychology of oral cultures and of the recitation of sacred scripture within those cultures is the place to begin this study. Recent studies of oral and literate cultures and of oral and written scripture provide a sound foundation for this work.[5] The areas that will need to be understood range from the styles and functions of oral recitation, the role of images in oral performance of sacred traditions, the relationship of written texts to the recital of the tradition, and the role of music in the sounds of the sacred traditions. That is, the texts will need to be exegeted against the background of their original context in terms of communications media and culture.

The foundation of the television Bible will be to understand the sounds and images of the texts themselves. This process will require new methods of exegetical study that will focus, first of all, on identifying the oral characteristics of the text in its original context. The units of speech will need to be identified. Where do the minor and major pauses occur? This is related to the concerns of rhetorical criticism but focuses on the sounds of the ancient texts. It will also be important to identify the mnemonic structures of the text.

Since one of the goals of the translation will be to make it as easy to remember as possible, the patterns of organization in the oral text that were intended to facilitate memory will need to be known. In order to even perceive these structures, it may be necessary to memorize the texts in their original languages. Furthermore, the text's rhythm, melody, volume and tempo will need to be identified as well as the elements of alliteration and assonance, parallelism, repetition, chiasm and the rhetorical appeals to the ancient audience. Only this redefined understanding of exegesis will provide an adequate foundation for an audio-video translation of the Bible. Until we know as much as possible about the sounds of the texts in their original context, we cannot translate them into the words and styles of contemporary languages and television styles.

This raises the question about how much we can actually know about the sounds of the ancient texts. We know relatively little, for example, about the precise pronunciation of ancient languages and the melodies for the cantillation of ancient sacred texts. While it may be impossible for us to know precisely how Greek and Hebrew were pronounced in the ancient world and the exact melodies that were used for a particular text, historical research is possible that will enable us to gain a more accurate understanding of the sounds of the ancient texts than we have at present. In relation to the melodies of ancient recital, a basic methodology for this study will be to compare the extant traditions of Hebrew and Greek cantillation and to reconstruct the sounds of the original sources from which these extant traditions developed.

The scholarship in this area has reached a significant degree of agreement that cantillation was an integral part of Christian and Jewish worship and education throughout the period of antiquity.[6] That is, we know that the scriptures were originally chanted in services of both synagogue and church. In view of recent research on oral poetry and narrative such as the studies of Lord and Perry, the probability is also high that this practice in the recital of the manuscripts continued in a formalized manner the spontaneous process of chanting that was characteristic of oral tradition.[7] Thus, we will need to know more about the sounds of the biblical tradition in order to accomplish an informed translation of the Bible into the sounds of our age.

Once this is known to a greater degree it will be possible to develop translations of the Bible using the melodies and harmonies that are more characteristic of modern civilization in electronic media. Thus, we need to develop a whole new series of translations of the Bible for recital rather than for study. Once this is accomplished we will also need to develop new ways of printing the texts that will indicate the units of sound in the translation. Thus, just as a primary task of scholarship has been to produce the best documentary form of the tradition, a new task is to produce the best electronic form of the tradition. It will be the correlate for an electronic age of Codex Vaticanus, the Masoretic text, the King James Bible, and whatever modern translation one thinks is best.

The investigation of the images of the texts is even more difficult. What are the appropriate visual components of biblical texts? At the first level this will involve the estimation of the visual components implicit in the experience of the original texts. One way of pursuing the question is to ask what the original audience actually saw. The images in the synagogues or catacombs as well as the faces of the reciter and the other listeners are possible visual elements. This might lead to dramatized recitals of the biblical texts in an ancient setting.

Another focus is to identify the images the text invites the audience to see in their imaginations. The representation of those images might be highly symbolic and fluid. Symbols, religious art in the tradition of two dimensional icons and three dimensional paintings, photographs and video montage, the sights of liturgy and worship, the faces of living persons, historical documentary footage: all are possible visual elements of Biblical texts. Answering this question will involve research into the history and theology of images and experimentation with a range of options.

THE DISTRIBUTION OF THE ELECTRONIC BIBLE

In every earlier media age after the original oral period, the production and distribution of the Bible has been done in a combination of ways. The most important form of distribution has been the oral recitation of the texts in public worship. But the production and distribution of biblical texts has steadily grown. As is evident from the book display at any meeting of biblical scholars, clergy or church conference, the community of biblical interpreters is presently organized to produce and distribute the Bible in the medium of print, primarily print intended to be read in silence. But when you consider all the materials about the Bible presently produced for use in the life of the churches, it comprises an immensely complex mix.

The task before us is to develop systems of production and distribution of the Bible in electronic media. The religious communities will be the primary source for these systems, but biblical scholars may need to take their own initiatives. To our knowledge there are no existing production houses or distribution agencies that have been persuaded of the need for an audio-video translation based on careful scholarship. Two major biblical video projects have been produced: the New Media Bible and the Hanna-Barbera series for children. Both have been commercial ventures with virtually no foundation in biblical scholarship or historical study.

For different reasons our evaluation of these projects is not positive. Both are flawed by basic decisions about format and by a lack of understanding or appreciation of the character of the Bible.

The New Media Bible transforms biblical narratives into a series of dramas. The Hanna-Barbera series is symbolized by its twentieth century children who enter the biblical situations via a time warp. The series is frequently highly anachronistic and steadily reads contemporary issues back into the texts in inappropriate ways. Only when the format of the project itself grows out of an understanding of the Bible in its original media context will there be the hope of an authentic translation. Only a production house and distribution system developed and owned by the church will have even the possibility of sufficient reverence for the Bible and its critical role in the church's mission to invest in such a new translation.

The conclusion is, therefore, that the production and distribution of the electronic Bible will need to be generated and controlled by the church. Only when the translation is conceived as an integral part of the church's thought and action will it be produced in a manner worthy of the Bible itself. The primary motivation for this project is to make the biblical tradition available to the television culture. However, the past sales record of both the Bible and related interpretive materials may help to support the vision, once viable projects are generated. In all probability, audio, video and computer Bibles will best be distributed with accompanying interpretive books. But biblical interpreters will have to fight to maintain integrity because of the complexity of the production and distribution systems needed to accomplish the task.

> **The development of narrative preaching and biblical storytelling... could only have happened in the context of the culture of the electronic age.**

In the previous periods of media change, the earlier systems of interpretation were continued and reformed in relation to the new paradigm. For example, the original oral traditions of the storytellers, prophets and psalmists were reformed for the culture of writing as texts which were read aloud in public readings and interpreted in doctrinal preaching and teaching. Thus, in the paradigm of the Bible in television, oral and written interpretation will be continued and reformed. New forms may emerge. For example, storytelling has experienced a renaissance in the culture and in biblical interpretation in the last ten years. The development of narrative preaching and biblical storytelling is a post-literate orality that could only have happened in the context of the culture of the electronic age. The character of books is also changing: e.g., fewer tomes, more short books, multiplication of specialized publications and journals. Therefore, the medium of interpretation of the electronic Bible will be a media mix of oral, written and electronic elements.

THE PROBLEM OF A HERMENEUTIC
FOR THE BIBLE ON TELEVISION

The most complex issue is the way in which meaningful connections will be made in television between the contemporary world and the world of the Bible. Media change is a major factor that has generally been unrecognized in the hermeneutical literature, including that of the "new" hermeneutic. What will be the hermeneutics of the electronic age? To this point the basic approach to the Bible on television has been to focus on the theological meaning of the texts.

The medium of communications establishes certain constraints that operate in the formation of meaning in that medium. In his **Preface to Plato** Eric Havelock has shown the way in which the transition from orality to literacy necessitated an epistemological revolution of separating the knower from what is known.[8] In the world of literacy one knows through reflecting on the ideas implicit in sense experience. Knowledge of the real world of the forms comes through reflection on sense experience. This primary revolution of the perception of sense experience as pointing beyond itself to transcendent ideas is an essential component of the world of literacy.

We would suggest that, in the tradition of biblical interpretation, this epistemological revolution associated with literacy was implemented in the development of theology as the primary hermeneutical system. In its various forms theology has been the way the Christian tradition has made connections between the contemporary world and the world of the Bible. The primary characteristic of theology is critical reflection on the ideas that are identified in the Bible. Theology as a hermeneutic has been based on the distinction between the phenomena of the Bible itself and the theological truths or noumena of which the Bible is the source.

The question in the context of the Bible and television is whether theology provides a viable hermeneutic in the sound and image medium of television. The depth of the problem is evident when theological discourse is taken from books and oral discourse and put on television. Imagine the grandeur and power of Paul Tillich's **Systematic Theology** or Karl Barth's **Church Dogmatics** on television or audio tape, or the fascination of Rudolf Bultmann's commentary on the Gospel of John in a televised exegetical discussion. Everyone recognizes that such program concepts will not work in the medium of television. A transmediazation of Thomas Aquinas' **Summa** is not a viable project for television. Yet the mainline churches have produced literally thousands of discussion programs in which the primary format was to bring together representatives of various points of view for a cordial theological discussion. The underlying assumption has been that the interpretive methods that were developed for writing will be equally appropriate for television.

In his chapter in this book on television as a medium for theology, Tyron Inbody has introduced a distinction that is foundational for constructive thinking about this problem. He distinguishes two orders of language about God. "First order" language is the broad category of the languages of faith and witness. These expressions include nonlinguistic idioms such as gestures, dance, music, art and architecture as well as talk about God. "First order" expression of faith and witness about God is found in the myths, stories, poetry, prayer, rhetoric, liturgy, hymns and dogmas of the church. By dogmas he refers to the primary language about God in Christian faith in the confessions of the church in which "I believe" is the characteristic introduction.[9] Theology is then "second order" language which reflects on the primary languages of faith.

There are two dimensions of this distinction that are helpful for this discussion. The first is the relationship between language and experience. "First order" or primary language is more closely related to experience. Many of the primary languages have a performative function. They are the languages in which things are done in the relationship with God and in the faith community, e.g., confession, praise, marriage and communion. The "second order" language of theology is a language of critical reflection that is detached from the immediacy of experience. In relation to television it is clear that the first order languages are more appropriate to the sounds and images of the medium. This does not mean that second order languages are inappropriate. As Inbody rightly argues in his chapter, the second order language of theology has an important role in the medium and culture of television.

The equally important contribution of Inbody's distinction is to clarify the relationship between the various languages in which the church talks about God. As he states, "Theology...is a dependent, derivative, second order language, reliant on the primary language of faith and witness."[10] The implication is that the very possibility of theology itself is dependent on the presence and vitality of the primary languages. Furthermore, one of the roles of theology is to reflect on the content and functions of the primary languages. Hence, narrative theology is critical reflection on the role of narrative in the church's talk about God.

What is then the character of the languages of the Bible? Is the Bible composed of the primary languages of faith and witness or is it critical reflection on the primary languages? The most prevalent language of the traditions of Israel and early Christianity is story; narrative comprises over half of both testaments. The traditions of prophecy and psalm are poetry and are closely related to the primary languages of proclamation and prayer. The wisdom tradition is primarily composed of proverbs and short sayings. Story, parable, proverbs, poetry, prophecy: all of these languages of the biblical tradition are primary languages.

In the paradigms of biblical interpretation in the world of writing and especially in the paradigm of silent print, the purpose has been to render the primary languages of the Bible into the secondary language of theology. The methods of biblical study have been designed to deconstruct the Bible as story, poetry, proverb and song and to reconstruct them in the form and language of theology. Thus, the most characteristic product of biblical criticism is biblical theology.

But, as Inbody's distinction helps to clarify, if we equate the Bible and its faithful interpretation with theology, we are limiting the languages for television to the secondary language of critical reflection. If we use the language and literature of theology as our norm for what is authentically bibli-

> **The most viable hermeneutic for the interpretation of the Bible on television is a narrative hermeneutic.**

cal, our approach to electronic media will be as if we would only broadcast literary, music and film critics on television and never have storytellers, musicians or athletes. Our only offering would be interminable, abstract discussions about stories, music and sports. Our framework of interpretation is then designed to yield information about the second-order language of the ideas of the tradition rather than the first-order language of story, song, proverb and prophecy.

Thus, the primary reason why historical critical scholarship has had virtually no impact on the interpretation of the Bible in the electronic media of radio, audio tape, film and television is that it is not designed for that purpose. The hermeneutics and methods of historical critical scholarship as currently practiced are designed for the transmediazation of the Bible into the communications world of silent print. Historical criticism is a paradigm for finding meaning in documents read in silence. To put it another way it will be difficult for us to interpret the biblical tradition in a medium of direct experience of sounds and images if our methods are intended to eliminate sounds and images from our experience. Therefore, we are experiencing a major discontinuity in communications paradigms.

If the primary languages which are closest to experience itself are most compatible with the medium of television and if theology is dependent on the presence and vitality of the primary languages, the first task of the church's work in television is to present the primary languages of the Bible itself. Indeed, the very possibility of doing theology in the medium is dependent on the presence of the primary languages.

A HERMENEUTIC FOR THE BIBLE ON TELEVISION

The general shape of a new hermeneutic for the Bible in television can be identified in this context. This can obviously only comprise an initial proposal. The only way in which it can be tested is by being used in the actual process of interpretation in the medium of television itself.

The first characteristic of this hermeneutic emerges from the distinction between primary and secondary languages. Because of the highly sensory character of the medium of television, the interpretation of the Bible in the medium will need to use the primary languages rather than secondary languages. Rather than the characteristic move in theological interpretation of moving from the primary language of the text to the secondary language of the **idea** implicit in the text, interpretation will be built by the use of primary languages. That is, instead of connecting the text with contemporary experience by identifying transcendental truths, this mode of interpretation will build a matrix of connections in the primary languages then and now.

At one level this principle is implicit in some aspects of contemporary Christian television. Most of the programs of the electronic church rely heavily on the primary languages of prayer, song/poetry and story. A program by Jerry Falwell, Robert Schuller or Jimmy Swaggart is linguistically similar. There are songs and hymns, personal stories as witness, prayer and sermon. With the possible exception of the sermon, these are all primary languages. One would need to add to this television list the new primary language of the appeal for money. But, at another level, while these languages are present, they are frequently only marginally used to interpret the Bible. In general the biblical content of these programs is minimal. The scriptures themselves are rarely presented and, if so, in very short texts that are primarily used as proof texts for whatever theme is being developed. Generally the Bible is interpreted in highly selective and anachronistic ways that have connected it with various American conservative causes such as getting rich, success in business, and the build-up of American military defense. Thus, while the programs of the electronic church demonstrate the viability of the use of the primary languages in the medium of television, they do not provide adequate models for the interpretation of the Bible in the medium.

In effect a hermeneutic of the primary languages involves a form of midrash or collection of commentaries. At the most basic level midrash sets stories, proverbs and laws from the contemporary context next to the traditional texts. A midrashic commentary involves making connections to the tradition by both analyzing the text and developing contemporary narrative, proverbial or legal traditions that grow naturally out of the text. But midrash is primarily composed of primary languages. Thus, in the broadest sense the proposal here is that a hermeneutic of the Bible for television can be based on a midrash of the primary languages.

The second dimension of a hermeneutic for the Bible in television emerges from a further analysis of the Bible itself. What is the structure of thought that underlies the biblical tradition? We tend to assume that the structure of biblical thought is theological. But this ignores the basic fact that, when seen in relation to Inbody's distinction, there are no secondary language works that are designed as critical reflection in the Bible.

All of the books of the Bible are written in the primary languages: e.g., story, poetry, prophecy and proverb. The closest to theology are the wisdom traditions of the Old Testament and the Pauline epistles of the New Testament. But the wisdom traditions of the Bible have a literary form and structure that is radically different from any theological essay. And Paul's letters are passionate and often chaotically organized discourses that were written for direct encounter with the congregations. The theological interpretation of the Bible is one of the characteristic products of the patristic period. Only the development of a full orbed allegorical method of interpretation by forbears such as Origen made it possible to deconstruct the narratives of the Bible into a philosophical/theological system.

But the primary structure of thought in the Bible was based on a narrative rather than a theological framework. The story of the actions of God, past, present and future, provided the basic structure of biblical thought. In fact, as is reflected in the liturgical years of Christianity and Judaism, that story of God has continued to provide the substructure of both Jewish and Christian thought.

The proposal here is, therefore, that the most viable hermeneutic for the interpretation of the Bible on television is a narrative hermeneutic. Thinking within the framework of the story of God leads naturally to the identification of the connection between the biblical experience of God and contemporary life. Rather than requiring the stepping back from experience that is the characteristic move of theology, a narrative hermeneutic invites a stepping into the connections between biblical and contemporary experience.

In the television productions of the major Protestant churches today, each major denomination has developed a program for the interpretation of their present programs. In the United Methodist

Church, for example, it is called "Catch the Spirit." This program is a storytelling program in which the stories of contemporary persons and communities are told. However, as far as we can discover none of the churches has developed any on-going programs of either biblical or theological interpretation. The development of a narrative hermeneutic for the interpretation of the Bible would open up the possibility of linking the story of God in the biblical tradition with the stories of the church's ministry now.

Thus, the outline of a paradigm for the Bible in television has the following components: the development of audio-visual translations based on an understanding of the sounds and images of the Bible; the combination of electronic, written and oral resources in a new media mix for the interpretation of the Bible; the formation of a church-owned distribution system; and a hermeneutic based on the primary rather than secondary languages and on a narrative structure of thought.

TYRON INBODY

"In most ways I'm part of the pre-baby boom generation. But I'm dumfounded by the number of students who don't know the novels, the movies and the television programs I refer to in my classes as illustrations of what I am talking about. So I guess I'm more a part of the television generation than I think I am."

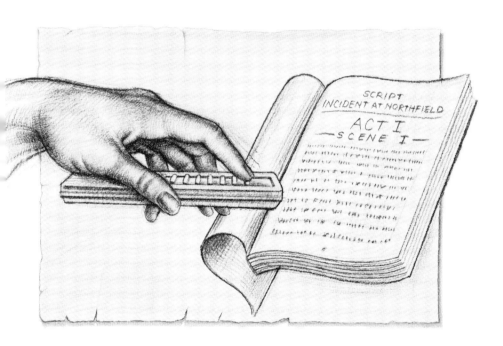

❝ *If I wrote for television I'd do docudramas. But I'd have a hard time finding music for them. That probably shows an inconsistency in my personality, because in some senses I think God quit writing music with Beethoven and Mozart.* ❞

"There is some contemporary music that I thoroughly enjoy. Not so much orchestral music, but some of the music my sons play, like Billy Joel, Elton John and Indigo Girls. A good friend of mine, Bill Dean, claims that if I really would listen to twentieth century symphonies, I would not find contemporary music as dissonant and chaotic as it seems to be. That's one of the symptoms, I guess, of my straddling the line between modern and postmodern. But I think the world and all of us in it are like that. We're both ordered and disordered, feeling and thinking, reasonable and irrational, good and bad."

"I now use images in class more than I did in the past. I'm not sure that's intentional. It probably has a lot to do with changes in me and in the culture in general. In this respect I would agree that television has had an impact on the way we think. At the same time I also want to insist upon the importance of critical analysis in what we do and say -- especially in the academy, but in other places as well. I am likely to defend the Enlightenment at the same time I criticize it, and to laud modernity as much as postmodernity. I don't understand those as either/or. I can both enjoy things and do hard analysis. This affects the way I teach as well as the content. I thoroughly enjoy the most critical work that I do in class, and I also do the most critical work of the things that I enjoy the most. I simply don't understand those as either/or. It frustrates my friends when I go to a movie and enjoy it and analyze it at the same time."

"I am not a dualistic thinker: I don't think in either/or categories. I am a both/and thinker. For me the glass is both half full and half empty. We're both bodies and minds. Distinctions don't necessarily mean separations."

"The place where I think there is the most promise for theology in the electronic media is the dispute. There are probably electronic forms of the medieval tradition of oral debates that can supplement the print version of theology all of us are trained in. I don't see contemporary expressions of the dispute that are particularly compelling at this point. But there are some possibilities on the horizon."

CHAPTER FOUR

TELEVISION AS A MEDIUM FOR THEOLOGY

Tyron Inbody

During the past century a new stage of verbal communications has dawned in the West. Electronic means of communications have supplemented orality, script and print. The earliest forms of this development were the telegraph and the telephone. Then electronic mass communications through radio and sound pictures were extended, following World War II, to television. In recent years video cassettes, cable, satellites, teletex, videotex, microwave circuits and computers have increased the ways people can converse through the electronic circuit.

This chapter explores the significance of television for the church and its theologians by examining the development of communications media, the role of media in the construction of a world, the character of modern theology and its relation to the print medium, the challenges to theology in a culture where television has become a dominant medium, and the possibilities for doing theology in a television culture. Can the church carry out its theological work in a culture whose parishioners, clergy, students and professors are significantly shaped by the medium of television?

The thesis is that the predominantly negative attitude most theologians have toward television as a medium of communications is not necessary. Theology is not inherently tied to one medium, and in a postmodern era it will be affected by the electronic media. There are characteristics and resources in theology as such which make that adaptation possible.

The argument is not that theology should substitute one medium for another. This author intends to keep reading theology books and writing theology papers until he dies, and he expects his students trained in theology to be able to do the same. Rather, the claim is that it is possible for theology to be done in and shaped by electronic media and still be theology. How that is to be done is the task to be explored by the new generation of theologians who are products of a television culture; that it can be done is the burden of the argument of this chapter.

DEVELOPMENT OF COMMUNICATIONS MEDIA

Communications media have a history. Walter Ong has traced the transformation of the word through three stages: from the preliterate, oral-aural stage, through script, which includes the substages of early script, alphabet manuscripts and the typographic word, to the electronic stage.[1] Thomas Boomershine follows a similar outline of development, but distinguishes between oral, manuscript, print, silent print and electronic means.[2]

Later stages of development do not cancel out earlier forms. Earlier forms persist, are built upon and are given new shape by later advances, as Quentin Schultze shows in his chapter. Oral-aural communication does not disappear in a print culture, and reading and writing continue to be used in an electronic culture. Indeed, oral-aural communication is a basic component of some electronic media, such as radio, and writing and print are required and even increased in other forms, such as the computer.

Nevertheless, there are significant consequences for a culture when media shift. Even though oral-aural forms persist in an electronic culture, there is a significant reorientation from a tribal to a global community as a result of electronic media. Styles of thinking are also affected. Greek philosophical thought was a new kind of thought released by an alphabetized culture. In Plato this new way of thinking took issue with and superceded the thought patterns of the oral-aural world of the poets of his day.

MEDIA AND WORLD CONSTRUCTION

Every human society is an enterprise in world building.[3] Unlike the other higher mammals, who are born with an essentially completed organism, human beings are unfinished at birth. We have to build a world for ourselves by imposing a meaningful order on our discrete experiences. Language is central in constructing this human world. It orders a world by imposing differentiation and structure on the ongoing flux of experience. In addition, it provides an order of relationships by the addition of syntax and grammar to vocabulary.

What is sometimes less recognized, however, is the role other elements of culture play in shaping this world order. The acquired order also depends on material products. Human beings manufacture tools. And once produced the tools have a logic of their own that also is internalized and shapes their users. A plow is an external object not only in the sense that its users employ it. The plow also compels its users to arrange their agricultural activity, and perhaps other aspects of their lives, in a way that conforms to its logic, ways not intended or foreseen by those who devised the plow.

One of the most important contributions of media studies is our increasing awareness of the subtle and profound effects media have on their producers and users. Although language is a fundamental factor in shaping the human world, it comes to us through a medium, and the medium of that language, whether it be oral or written, heard or seen, print or electronic, is important in shaping its meaning and the kind of world it creates.

What kinds of effects do the electronic media have on us and the world we continually create and recreate? The new configurations of language, sight and sound, electronic image, split second speed and universal availability cast a different world than the world oral-aural and print media mold.

One does not need to be a "technological determinist" or a "one factor" interpreter to recognize that innovations in communications technologies have important consequences for our perception of the world. Technology itself affects world construction. There is a significant difference between the spoken word and the alphabet, between speech and writing. Walter Ong points out that in an oral-aural culture memory is more thematic and formulaic, whereas in an alphabet culture records are more visual and sequential. Phonetic literacy divides experience up into linear sequence. The "message" of this particular medium, McLuhan argues, is individuality, the continuity of space and time and uniformity of codes. Literacy produces privacy, fragmentation, division, the repeatable, the point of view and the specialist. Even the idea of reason is affected by the alphabet and its alliance with the technologies of manuscript and print. "Neither Hume nor Kant . . . detected the hidden cause of our Western bias toward sequence as 'logic' in the all-pervasive technology of the alphabet."[4]

> **Modern theology has tended to be 'medium dependent' if not 'medium specific'.**

With the appearance of electronic technology, we extend not simply our physical organs but our central nervous systems. "By imposing unvisualizable relationships that are the result of instant speed, electric technology dethrones the visual sense and restores us to the dominion of synesthesia, and the close interinvolvement of the other senses."[5] Just as the central nervous system is a unified field without segments, so this new technology is organic in character. The speed of involvement creates a total field of interacting events in which people participate.

The electronic medium tends to present an organic and non-mechanical message. Electronic communication favors the inclusive and the participational spoken word and the image over against the specialist written word. In this respect the new technology has more affinity to the oral and tribal ear than to the literate eye. In television the visual linear mode of perception is reduced and tends to be supplanted by the more organic interinvolvement of sight, sound, speed and image. The phonetic alphabet and typographic print, which have been decisive factors in the shaping of "the modern mind," now exist along side a medium which is reshaping our perceptions of reality.

The print medium will not disappear in the postmodern world. The perception of reality and the skills made available through it are no less influential in the new stage of communications development than is oral-aural communication in a print culture. Nevertheless, the problem for a print culture is not merely "it's how we use the new medium that counts." Postmodern culture will have to learn how to understand and to respond to the world shaping power of the new medium as well.

How should the mainline churches and modern theology, products in part of a literate culture which has access to mass media print, respond to the new electronic media? Are they to become enclaves of one stage of communications development? Or can the mainline churches and their theologians supplement and reshape their understanding of theology within a culture that constructs its world as much through television as through the printed word?

MODERN THEOLOGY AS CRITICAL REFLECTION

What is theology? Theology, literally, is *logos* about *theos*; it is thought and speech about God. Christian theology is talk about God based in the church's witness to God in Jesus Christ. Theology is dependent upon the antecedent reality of revelation and witness. In order to grasp the distinctive character of theology, though, it is necessary to recognize that one can distinguish theology and faith without separating them. They are essentially connected yet distinct.

Faith itself is an existential reality. It has prelinguistic and even preconscious (subconscious and unconscious) features to it, such as awe, the sense of holiness, the feeling of absolute dependence, appreciative awareness, confidence in the meaningfulness of life, or what Santayana called "animal faith."

In addition faith and its witness can be expressed in many nonlinguistic idioms, such as gestures, dance, play, music, art and architecture. Genuflecting, rising for the Gospel lesson, moving to the table, sitting before a stained glass window, and roving the dark and musty isles of a cathedral are more elemental and primary expressions of faith and witness than talk about God.

Furthermore, not all talk about God is theology. Human beings express their faith and witness verbally through myths, stories, poetry, prayer, rhetoric and dogmas. Indeed, the primary language about God in Christian faith is the language of the confessions, namely, "Jesus Christ is Lord," "Jesus is the Christ," and "I believe in God the Father.... and in Jesus Christ.... and in the Holy Spirit." These primary confessions of faith, and other linguistic forms of witness in scripture, liturgy and hymns, constitute the "first order" language of faith. They are the primary linguistic forms of the Christian witness and provide the subject matter of theology proper. Theology, therefore, is a dependent, derivative, "second order" language, reliant on the primary language of faith and witness.

Theology is the kind of thought and speech about God which is engaged in critical reflection on the witness of faith. It is a reflexive discipline. When the primary language of faith, and its close language of verbal image, metaphor and myth become unclear, doubtful or debatable because the first order language of the believer is challenged by other witnesses of faith or because the believer herself is uncertain or needs to correlate Christian witness with new perceptions of reality, theology proper arises to provide critical reflection upon faith in order to help the believer meet these needs and challenges. In performing this specific task theology must be distinguished from faith as a strictly "second order" language in the service of the "first order" language of witness. "Theology is **about** what we must say to be saying the gospel; it is a second-order activity over against the actual speaking of the gospel."[6]

Although there is widespread agreement among contemporary theologians about the definition of theology as critical reflection, there are differences about how to comprehend and pursue critical reflection. One divergence is between those who understand theology to be devoted to the philosophical questions of the meaning and truth of faith approached through philosophical analysis, and those who conceive it to be devoted to a broader range of problems and who seek to understand Christian witness by employing a wide variety of analytical disciplines.

Among contemporary theologians Schubert Ogden is the most consistent advocate and representative of the first group. Theology proper is the fully reflective understanding of the Christian witness of faith as decisive for human existence according to the twin criteria of appropriateness to the gospel and credibility in light of the relevant conditions of truth universally established with human existence.[7] Theology, specifically, is the critical discipline of thought devoted to the specific questions of the meaning and truth of the Christian faith in the light of these dual criteria. Although theology, which encompasses historical, systematic and practical reflection, is not itself restricted to any one particular philosophical system or to philosophy itself, it must, to be fully reflective, address the philosophical problems of the cognitive meaning and truth of the Christian witness.

This definition of theology has led Ogden to conclude that many forms of contemporary theology are not theology proper but rather are forms of Christian witness. For example, much of the current liberation theology is "thought and speech about God in general" and not critical reflection on the problems of the meaning and truth of our talk about God according to the proper criteria of theology.[8]

Ogden acknowledges, however, that "how Christian theology should understand itself. . . remains among the most controversial theological questions."[9] Among contemporary theologians there is another group which defines theology more broadly as "intentional Christian thinking about important questions or issues."[10] Theology is intentional, disciplined and critical thinking about a wide range of important concerns to Christian faith. Within this perspective the various liberation theologies are as fully theological as are philosophical theologies, as are the theologies which explore metaphor and narrative as expressions of the meaning and truth of Christian faith.[11]

What is crucial is the recognition that, regardless of whether one understands theology according to the narrower limits or the broader parameters, theology is understood by all those who claim to be engaged in it to be critical reflection upon Christian faith and witness.

Thus, James Cone, a Black liberation theologian, says,

> Christian theology . . . is the rational study of the being of God in the world in light of the existential situation of an oppressed community. . . . This means that its sole reason for existence is to put into ordered speech the meaning of God's activity in the world, so that the community of the oppressed will recognize that their inner thrust for liberation is not only consistent with the gospel but is the gospel of Jesus Christ.[12]

Rosemary Ruether, a liberation and feminist theologian, agrees.

> Theology is the critical reflection upon the praxis of human liberation. This is liberation theology's definition of theology's "role." . . . But theology is not to be merely critical. It is also to be reflection upon constructive activity. This means that theology does not exist as a system of thought that can be an end in itself. Rather it must be in a constant process of hermeneutical translation into the concrete situation of preaching, mission, building up of the community. It mediates and reflects upon this activity as its life blood.[13]

And Sallie McFague, who conceives of narrative theology as an "intermediary theology" existing on a continuum between parable and systematic theology, thinks of theology "as a second-order level of reflection upon the parabolic forms of the poem, novel, and autobiography."[14] Her theory is that the primary religious language is image, parable, metaphor and story. From these emerge poetry, novels and autobiography. Finally, "a variety of reflective forms" follows, conceptual interpretation and criticism of constructive theology being but one form of critical understanding, of moving beyond the primary images and metaphors of faith in order to avoid literalizing them.[15]

What is common and essential to all of these conceptions of theology is the notion of critical reflection. The theologian stands back at some distance from the primary language of faith and employs the language of analysis in order to come to a critical understanding of Christian witness and practice. The difference is that the latter group includes a broader range of analytical tasks and frameworks in what is considered to be the kind of "critical reflection" that is appropriate to theology proper.

> **Television seems not to be conducive to the dissemination and discussion of ideas.**

The first group employs the questions and methods of philosophical analysis, including metaphysics, existentialist analysis and linguistic usage. The second group, depending on the perspective employed, uses Marxist analysis, sociology of knowledge, ideology critique, historical reconstruction, and contemporary literary and hermeneutical theory as their principles of criticism. What all of them share in common, however, is the insistence on critical thinking as the essential characteristic of theology proper. It is accurate to say that all modern theologians, regardless of other fundamental differences, understand and practice theology as critical reflection upon Christian faith, witness and practice.

By identifying theology with the critical task, we tie modern theology closely to analysis, to the power of the mind to penetrate, take apart and grasp the relationships that constitute the object of study. Understanding depends on the capacity of the mind to analyze.

What sometimes escapes the modern critical mind, however, is an awareness of the way in which modern understanding is affected by the medium which is employed through which to carry out the analysis. The phonetic alphabet in general and the print medium in particular, that is, literacy in the modern sense of the term, is an ingredient in the concept of theology as critical reflection. Modern theology has tended to be "medium dependent" if not "medium specific." Its definition has been shaped by the logic of understanding configured by the print medium. Not only is it impossible to conceive of theology apart from some notion of critical thinking; it is difficult to think of critical reflection as modern theology practices it apart from literacy and the print medium. The mode of thinking in modern theology is in part bequeathed to it by the logic inherent in the primary medium it employs to carry out its work. It is, at least in part, dependent upon the visual, perspectival, analytical, linear and sequential thinking of its dominant medium.

THE CASE AGAINST TELEVISION
AS A MEDIUM FOR THEOLOGY

If theology is understood to be a body of information, a fixed set of doctrines and dogmas to be transmitted to an audience, television is probably an effective means to convey this information to a mass audience. But if theology is critical reflection upon faith and witness, there are some questions to consider before theologians attempt to employ television as a medium for their work as theologian. These questions are deeper than how to use the medium to educate people about theological ideas. The question is whether the goals of the theologian are compatible with the primary characteristics of the medium.

Both the academic community and the churches, on the whole, have been skeptical about television as a medium for analysis. Some of the most significant criticism from the churches is that 1) the medium of broadcast television is closed and controlled by the economic and political ideology of elites who use it as the most efficient and effective means by which to reinforce their interests, 2) the worldview and values the medium inculcates, namely, that human beings are essentially consumers, constitute a perspective which stands counter to the Christian view of humanity, and 3) the conservative Protestant churches, who have adopted the medium, have unwittingly accepted the American mythos of technological progress without recognizing the subtleties and complexities of communications or the communal character of the church.[16]

In addition to the medium of television being a cultural institution by which groups negotiate, with more or less power, their place within a society, however, the medium is also a technology which itself helps to frame the meanings of a culture. This is not to claim an ahistorical or deterministic view of technology. It is, however, to acknowledge that there is a mutual interrelation between institution and technology. The definitions of meaning and truth are derived in part from the character of the medium of communication itself. Thus, evaluating "medium as epistemology" is as important as evaluating television as "ideology" (bourgeois institution) or television as "junk" (aesthetic degradation).

The dilemma can be clearly stated. Television, because of characteristics of the medium itself, seems not to be conducive to the dissemination and discussion of ideas. But reflection upon ideas is central and even essential to the very concept of theology proper.

Television is in basic ways a non-reflective medium. It is most adept at the creation and manipulation of images. This is not merely what television does best; it is what it does by the logic of the medium itself, quite independent of any benevolent or malevolent intentions of its creators or institutional users. Television, because of the kind of balance it creates between the auditory and visual senses, washes away the rigorous separation and specialization of the senses of "the typographic mind"[17] where the visual sense and the linear mode are at the top of the hierarchy.

Modern theology is in decisive ways a child of typography, but television has reshaped our senses and our mental processes in a new ratio of speed, auditory and visual experience, substituting for the clash of ideas and viewpoints in the print medium depth involvement in the image itself. Television is less suited to subtle controversial topics. It serves better our taste for participation in depth in an image or a narrative or a conflict.

What we are suggesting is that the practice and training for critical thinking, which stands at the center of theology and is one of the main purposes of theological education in the modern period, is increasingly difficult to accomplish and defend in an electronic era. The logic of the electronic media has shaped the experience and thought of most theological students today, and it competes increasingly with the logic of the print medium and the kind of critical thinking characteristic of that medium. The theological seminary is at the point where it must decide whether to respond to the electronic age by retreating to a specialization model, that is, to claim that its role is to represent the kind of critical thinking that has been shaped by print media and to criticize the content of television and how it is used, or to explore ways theological education can broaden its task to include the ways we experience and think in the medium of television.

The answer to this question is bound to be controversial. The reason is that the pressure inherent in television both as a social institution and as a technology is to exchange critical reflection, the dominant mode of thinking in modern theology and theological education, for another form of discourse. Notions of information, thinking, knowledge and truth take on new meanings. Neil Postman notes that "[t]elevision . . . does not direct our attention to ideas, which are abstract, sequential, slow-moving, and complex. It directs us to respond to images, which are holistic, concrete, and simplistic. That is why it rarely matters what anyone says on television."[18] Critical reflection is not promoted by the medium of television. Quite beyond the vested interests of owners and advertisers, arguments and counterarguments, scrutiny of assumptions, explanations, elaborations and definitions tend not to play well on television.

It is not the size of the screen and the time constraints alone which work against this kind of thinking. The fragmented and discontinuous sequence of images also contribute to this constraint. "[T]hinking does not play well on television. There is not much to see in it. It is, in a phrase, not a performing art."[19]

On television information is not primarily propositions to be judged true or false. Information is an image, and the truth or falsity of the "claim" is simply not an issue. The television advertisement, which is what television was revived for after the Second World War, is the quintessential example. The commercial is not a series of testable, logically ordered assertions. It is some variation of a drama of beautiful, happy people drinking Pepsi at Huntington Beach. "Is this a claim? Is this true or false? I submit that such questions do not apply to the world of visual images. One can like or dislike a television advertisement, but one cannot refute it."[20]

Primacy belongs to the picture, not to the idea, in politics and religion on television. Information is not a concept but a visual image and so is not subject either to logical analysis or refutation. The brain is replaced by the viscera. In such a world knowing means having pictures more than having sentences in your head. The image, embedded in a variety of formats, becomes the basic unit of public conversation. In such a context critical public discourse is both difficult and irrelevant. "Americans no longer talk to each other; they entertain each other. They do not exchange ideas; they exchange images. They do not argue with propositions; they argue with good looks, celebrities, parables, and public opinion polls."[21] The act of critical thinking as a detached, abstract, sequential mode of discourse does not play well in a medium whose logic is primarily the power of the image to totally involve the participant in an experience.

Our point is not that television is necessarily the enemy of rational discourse. There are counter examples, not only on public television and some cable channels but also on commercial broadcast television, which show that television not only can display events but can analyze them. "The McNeil-Lehrer Newshour" and William F. Buckley's "Firing Line" on public television, and Ted Koppel's "Nightline" on commercial television show that a discussion of ideas is possible in the medium. Nor is our purpose to argue that theological schools should not train students to interpret and critique television as an institution or the content of television programming on moral and aesthetic grounds.

Our claim is that the medium as such has a tendency to displace reflective thinking with other modes of experience and thought. Insofar as this is the case it does not appear to be a "user friendly" medium for theology. As Robert Bruinsma says in his review of Neil

Postman's views,

> "Of all the enemies of TV-teaching, none is more formidable than exposition. Arguments, hypotheses, discussions, reasons, refutations, or any of the components of reasoned discourse turn television into radio or, worse, third-rate printed matter. Thus television always takes the form of storytelling, conducted by dynamic images and supported by music. Thus television is inherently moralistic and value-laden because narratives of any kind -- in this case picture stories -- are inevitably aphoristic and metaphorical. Exposition, on the other hand, works through definition, assertion, explication, and analysis -- an ensemble that in contrast with the TV form of narration is relatively value-neutral."[22]

It tends not to provide grounds for conceptual, segmented, linear modes of expression, grounds for debate or ambiguity. And these are fundamental characteristics of modern theology.

If this analysis is correct it is by no means to argue the end of theology. Even if we are becoming an electronic culture, individuals and subcultures, such as disciplinary specialists in the schools who maintain the skills and thought forms of print media, will continue and contribute to the richness of our culture. There still will be room and a need for the school as "the alternative curriculum with its subject-matter, word-centered, reason-centered, future-centered, hierarchical, secular, socializing, segmented, and coherent curriculum."[23]

However, even though the dominance of television in our culture does present a challenge to theology and the education of theological students in the postmodern context, the confrontation of media cultures does not need to be resolved merely by a live-and-let-live attitude of isolation. It is time to explore the possibility that theology can be conceived in such a way that it might also employ the medium of television along with the text book in its work of critical reflection.

THE POSSIBILITY OF TELEVISION
AS A MEDIUM FOR THEOLOGY

Is it possible that television, whether through network broadcast, cable, closed circuit or video cassettes, might become a medium in which theologians can work? Or is theology so identified with the type of thinking characteristic of the print medium that it can only criticize the institution and the content of television from its distinctive point of view but cannot employ television, electronically produced visual images coupled with sound, as a medium in which to reflect critically on the Christian faith?

Although this chapter does not propose ways in which theology can be done on television, we want to explore the claim that it is possible for television to become a medium for theological thought to be used alongside the long established medium of print.

First, we consider the role of the image in theology. Although there are significant differences between print and electronic media, the difference is not absolute. In addition to the dominance of the image in the arts and television, the image plays a decisive role in theology as well.

Philosophical and systematic theology, for example, do not exist apart from determining images. Even though discursive analysis differs from aesthetic insight in clarity and precision of concepts, the critical mind cannot operate apart from formative images as primary data and shaping insight. The point is not only that theology speaks metaphorically and analogically about its subject matter, but that the critical mode of thought itself is dependent upon foundational images by which to understand the world. Although critical theology may not use images in the same way and for the same purposes that television images are used in the institution and medium in its present form, critical thinking which is shaped by the print medium also employs images.

> **Postmodern theologies have more affinity with the world of the electronic media.**

In order to illustrate this claim we might examine more closely the intelectual discipline which traditionally has claimed to be the most critical (that is, which provides the most abstract and universal concepts by which one can understand the world), namely, speculative philosophy. Metaphysics has claimed to be the "meta-critical discipline," and in terms of generality of concept and universality of application it is just that. Yet every system of speculative philosophy is rooted in an image which provides the primary insight through which one constructs the structure of reality. Systems of speculative philosophy, which provide the framework for many philosophical theologies, are based on a fundamental "judgement of importance."[24]

Some element of human experience is selected as the key image through which to render a rational interpretation of the world. Before reason can be employed to develop a coherent scheme of concepts, a prior judgement about the most relevant aspect of the world which provides the controlling image for the vision must be made. Plato, for example, found his image in the beauty of intelligible forms; Aristotle, in tracing the processes of biological development; Hegel, in the unfolding of the inner life of the mind; Hume, in sense experience; Whitehead, in organismic relations and the new physics.

In each case a basic image provides the metaphor which becomes a model by which the thinker can produce a set of categories and principles through which conceptually to understand the world. Indeed, to be "rational" means to apply the image and its elaboration through general categories and principles to every aspect of reality. The same procedure operates in theology itself. Theology depends on "root metaphors," such as creation, covenant, redemption, forgiveness, cross and resurrection, which grasp what is primordial in Christian experience and project it into a vast drama.

Furthermore, there is an affinity between television and theology in the narrative quality of each. Much of what is on television is narrative, and that structure of experience is what this particular medium excels in portraying. But much of theology, particularly theology from Augustine through contemporary narrative theology, has been narrative in basic structure, that is, an expression and interpretation in conceptual form of the story of creation, fall, election, redemption and fulfillment. This historical-narrative structure has been understood to be essential to the truth of Christian witness and theology.

Second, although theology is critical reflection upon Christian faith, historically considered critical thinking is not equated with texts, at least not to the degree that modern theology has equated theology with the printed word. Walter Ong points out that although in the Middle Ages and in the Renaissance theology was clearly more text oriented than in antiquity, theology was nevertheless thought to be as much an oral-aural discourse as it was thought to be textual.[25] Theology was rhetorical; it was carried on by means of the dispute. Theology was as much the art of discourse as it was pure logic, and the art consisted as much of dialectical exchange in the debate as it did of mastery of texts and production of more texts.

What happened with the development of the modern world, especially with Descartes, is that the art of thinking replaced the art of discourse. The medium of print and the logic of personal inquiry and the isolated thinker ousted the vocal exchange and its dialectic. Language came to belong to writing and not to speaking. Theology followed along with this development by identifying theology with the printed word and the kind of thinking shaped by print. If theology can be thought of again as critical thinking belonging as much to the oral-aural world of dispute as to the print world of critical analysis of the ideas of a text, then television might become a medium in which theology proper can be pursued.

Television is a natural medium for the oral-aural world of disputation. Certain features of critical thinking in the modern sense of the world are obscured or difficult to achieve within the medium of television, but one important form of critical thinking is not precluded. Theologians may be able to revive and reformulate the dispute or the debate as a form of critical thinking which is naturally effective in the medium of television.

We are not talking here about television as commercial broadcast for entertainment and advertisement. We are talking about a form of critical reflection in a medium which supplements the dominant medium used by theologians for critical thought for centuries. Television as video is ready-made for imaginative use for the oral-aural dispute.

Third, what may be threatening to theologians with the appearance of the new media is not so much the challenge to theology itself but to modern theology. Modern theologies have tended to be based on the Cartesian-Kantian notion of critique and on the Newtonian image of the machine and the mechanistic model of the world which followed from this image. Modern theologians are less likely to find possibilities for reflection in a world created by the electronic media than

❝The narrative theologican might find [television] to be an effective medium through which to explore the many levels of meaning in the community's story.❞

the postmodern theologies whose informative images and models are more organismic, inter-relational, metaphorical and narrative. Postmodern theologies have more affinity with the world of the electronic media.

There are, for example, the metaphorical and narrative as well as deconstructive theologies which have located the resources of theology and the reflective task more in the world of images and stories than in the world of concepts and abstractions. Various postmodern theologians have shown that, in addition to the self as thinker and actor, in addition to subjective consciousness as the normative human activity, our use of the image, with its power to form our perception of ourselves and our world through habitual attention, is as persuasive and is as subject to critical training, as is our use of language, with its power to anticipate and analyze our misunderstanding of the self and the world. Since television is the medium above all that mixes eye and ear, image and language in a new way, it is a medium in which criticism and training both for the perceptions and conceptions of Christian witness and understanding can be explored in a new context.

Television is also a medium in which theology as metaphor might be explored. Sallie McFague has argued that metaphorical theology stands somewhere between the primary religious language of image, parable, metaphor and story, which are the immediate expression of faith, on the one hand, and the secondary, fully reflective language of constructive or systematic theology.[26] Between the metaphor and abstract discourse stand certain theological forms of poetry, novels and autobiography, which have as their task to explore not the problem of translating the primary symbols into contemporary reflective language but of saying what is conceptually less perceivable and expressible. Bernard Meland proposes a similar concept of theology by distinguishing between theological discourse and theological inquiry, the former being more imaginative and the latter more definitive. Thus, theology is a mediate form of discourse between art and philosophy.[27]

Television may be less effective than print in analyzing the primary images and metaphors in strict second order language. But it may be more capable than some forms of print in conveying a wider range of the meanings of the primary religious language through a reflective and effective use of images, metaphors, novels and autobiographies by its novel blend of eye and ear, image and language.

In addition television has shown a capacity to perform not only primary religious functions of world building in a secular age through the use of images and rituals to constitute and maintain a world of shared beliefs and behaviors. It has also shown, inadvertently perhaps, a capacity to perform the critical task of analysis and judgement through its iconoclastic power to expose false powers, as in documentaries, hearings, news broadcasts and comedies.[28]

Potentially, one of the most fruitful explorations in the relation of television and theology is the link between medium and narrative theology. Narrative theologians are concerned with fables, myths, biographies and autobiographies as both source and subject of theological reflection. They "show regard for and give heed to those linguistic structures which, through their portrayal of the contingent interaction between persons and events, constitute the source and ground of such beliefs."[29] In performing the critical task of elucidating, examining and transforming these beliefs, the narrative theologian shows how the stories of the community give rise and shape to the life and beliefs of the community.

Television is not only an effective medium for portraying the various narratives that shape a community. Because of its capacity to explore a range of meanings through its unique blend of visual image and language, the narrative theologian might find it to be an effective medium through which to explore the many levels of meaning in the community's story. Television is not inherently restricted to creating images and portraying stories of human beings as consumers. It can critically explore a range of alternative images and a depth of meanings available in our culture, including those inherent in the Christian witness and faith. This may, in the end, be the most promising link between the theologian and television.

CONCLUSIONS

The first conclusion we suggest, then, is that the difference between philosophical theology and metaphorical theology is not that one of these alone is properly called theology, but that the form of argument and understanding in each is different. Images and stories remain, but the perspectives for understanding them vary. Every form of theological argument deals with the plausibility of the community's set of beliefs. Whereas a philosophical theology attempts to understand these within a logically coherent conceptual scheme, a metaphorical theology attempts to understand the beliefs from the perspective of how they emerge out of the invitational, participatory and performative roles of the images, metaphors and narratives that establish the world and the life of the community. These are not mutually exclusive or superior/inferior modes of reflection. Each serves the critical task of understanding the church's witness and faith.

The second conclusion we suggest is that theology, even when conceived properly as critical reflection, is not tied exclusively to one medium. It cannot be identified exhaustively with the kind of critical thought shaped by print culture. Other modes of critical reflection are available. Although the response of many thoughtful people has been to prefer "the elimination of television" because of the form the institution has taken in our culture to date, in both its secular and religious versions, and because of the biases of the medium as a technology against certain values of modern culture, theologians nevertheless have good reasons to think that the medium has possibilities for use by the church in a broad range of its tasks, including its theological tasks. The churches and seminaries should explore this possibility before they opt exclusively for the media forms of print culture and abandon the newer forms either to consumer exploitation by commercial interest groups or to the thoughtless banality or distortions of the gospel by the electronic church.

PAMELA MITCHELL

"I also grew up in the music generation. Sometimes I sit down and listen to the radio; sometimes I sit down and listen to records. Some forms of popular music I simply can't relate to. But there are also some forms that sweep me up. As a professional Christian educator I listen to music, particularly songs that might be of interest to youth. So I intentionally sit and listen a lot."

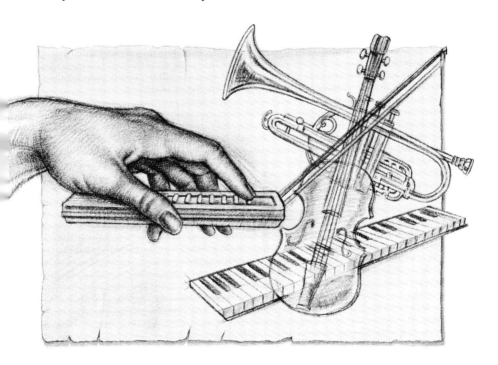

❝ *If I were given all the money I needed and could produce whatever new I wanted, I would do music video television. MTV has gotten destructively homogenous, and there is some really good music out there now. Some exciting new stuff with videos is waiting to be done.* **❞**

"Television is an important part of my generation. I grew up watching Mickey Mouse and Howdy Doody. Television forms a story base for me. It is not foreign or alien to me."

"I don't feel guilty at all when sitting in front of the tube. As an undergraduate major in film and media criticism, I am supposed to do this. Now I get paid to do it. It is my job, my responsibility, my duty! So I usually watch with two things in mind. One eye watches as pure criticism. The other eye watches as a teacher for what I can use in my teaching. But I rarely watch just for fun."

"The biggest effect television has on my work is on my teaching methods. I use television programs as case studies in the classroom because the characterizations work better than reading a case study. The media does not affect me in the sense that I think my teaching has to be entertaining, or that everybody's attention span is only four minutes long. Using television is primarily a method for me, a technique for accomplishing what I want to accomplish in class. My role as a teacher and scholar does alter the way I view television. I look at it as a teacher rather than as a visual critic of the medium. I watch everything with an eye toward how can I use this in class."

"I hope that the church can sing on television. But there is a real danger in assuming that this means the church should primarily be producing new things for television. I lean much more toward making use of what is already there instead of adding more to the pile that already exists. It is in the usage that the church can employ television, not necessarily in the church producing for it."

CHAPTER FIVE

APPROACHES TO TELEVISION IN RELIGIOUS EDUCATION

Pamela Mitchell

"What is there to say about television? At times it seems that the entire culture revolves around the images and sounds that emanate from the television screen, that all talk is somehow television talk."[1]

THREE SCENARIOS

Consider these three scenarios. First, you are about to take over as teacher of the Senior High Sunday School class in your church next quarter, so this week you are "sitting in" on the class to observe what they have been studying. The class has just finished watching an episode of "Different World," and the teacher has given each student a list with the following instructions: "Underline the eight qualities most evident in the main character in this show. Now think of someone you know personally whom you respect and admire. Circle eight things on the list that describe this person." The class uses this data to move into a discussion of television's portrayal of life in relation to life as the learners experience it.[2]

Second, you have joined a Sunday evening study/discussion group at your church. Tonight the group has seen the film *Cocoon*, and has settled down with coffee to discuss these questions: "What adjectives would you use to describe the older adults in this film? Is it proper for human beings to 'reshuffle the deck that nature has dealt,' as one character in *Cocoon* states? Most Americans believe in some form of life after death. What are the religious implications of the ending of *Cocoon*?"[3]

Third, your ten-year-old has just come home from Sunday School with a letter telling you about a "no television" experiment her class is undertaking. You are invited to a celebration to kick off two weeks of television-free living that the kids are voluntarily beginning. Your daughter tells you about books and games she wants to get during the experiment.

What is happening in the three churches described above? What is going on in these religious education programs? All three are responding to the presence of television as an influence in our culture, but they are responding in decidedly different ways. How can we understand what is taking place in each of these education programs, sort out our own positions, and choose the educational path appropriate for the church?

Each of the religious education programs described above is an example of the church's response to television. The very existence of these educational programs assumes that television is in some way an important or notable element in our lives, worthy and in need of address by the church. Why do these and other program resources exist? Although they differ in many respects, they share a focus on television as a cultural parameter and an understanding of the church's educational ministry as a way to approach, understand and develop responses to this culture.

This chapter will help answer these questions by addressing three topics: 1) the role of television in our culture, and why it is one focal point of concern for the church today, 2) the role of religious education as a ministry of the church, especially in relation to television, 3) the five different types of religious education that relate to television, including the underlying attitudes and assumptions of each type, and the specific methods of teaching employed.

POPULAR CULTURE AS TELEVISION CULTURE

In the latter half of the twentieth century, the church's response to culture has increasingly been focused on what has been called "popular culture," or "mass culture." Increasingly, this popular culture has become identified with the media that influence, communicate and depict that culture, so that popular culture can in some ways be called mass media culture. The presupposition is: **late twentieth century Christians must relate to a mass media culture.** Simply stated our culture is a mass media culture; it is to that culture we must connect.

The designation of our particular world as "mass media culture" is rooted in Walter Ong's distinctions between oral, literate and electronic mass media cultures.[4] For Ong cultures can be described in terms of the dominant communications mode, which shapes and affects tangible and intangible features of the culture.

In oral culture, the mode of existence for pre-printing societies, words are events or happenings. Words themselves move through and exist in time, rather than function as static records of events. Language is a real event, not a once-removed depiction of or reflection on an event. In this culture the only way to record or hold onto meanings is through personal and communal memory. Memory is not an external place or record, but is a part of persons; all that persons know, and all that has happened to them, is carried with them as part of them. To "know" is to remember. These memories become part of the community as they are shared through the event of words; speech is the event of sharing meanings that are part of persons. Communication is a direct, personal sharing of the self, and the culture is organized around the interpersonal interactions that create shared meaning. In the oral culture of Israel the knowledge of the people's heritage is a living memory communicated through the telling of the Exodus story. Persons know who they are through the story, repeated in home and tribal rituals.[5]

As alphabets and writing develop and literate culture joins oral culture, words no longer exist solely as events or within persons. Words become ways of encoding and storing events as records that can be visually engaged at will. No longer is access to words only available through direct access to persons. The words themselves become objects with which persons can have

"Television has become our informer, our metaphor builder, the background for our lives."

direct, unmediated contact. Ong says, "Writing establishes what has been called 'context-free' language or 'autonomous' discourse, discourse which cannot be directly questioned or contested as oral speech can be, because written discourse has been detached from its author."[6] Knowledge and meaning become part of the written record, rather than part of persons' memories and being.

Communication includes textual recording and interpretation, preserving and ferreting out precise meaning. Consequently, communication becomes more objective, impersonal and focused on words as objects. Direct personal involvement with others is no longer the necessary and sufficient basis of culture, since shared meaning is available through creating, maintaining and engaging objects. The developing characterization of Christians as "people of the book" demonstrates this point. As Thomas Boomershine shows the Bible came to be a book read silently and individually, in contrast to the communal sharing of stories in oral cultures.

Mass media culture encompasses oral and written communication, but reaches a new stage when a third form of communication, electronic, is added. For Ong mass media culture reaches its zenith when electronic technology combines the visual nature of literate culture with the aural nature of oral culture.

This is the culture in which most Western, late twentieth century Christians exist. In this culture some aspects of pre-literate oral culture are recovered, but they are transformed by the electronic media. Communications may once again be communal rather than individual objective engagement with texts,[7] but the community of discourse is no longer the tribe, within which individuals directly contact one another. The community within which we communicate is now global, and everyone everywhere can be present at once, yet not directly present in body. Nor can all of the meanings met in this exchange become a part of the persons involved; there are too many communications and too much complexity for a solid body of communal memory and meaning to be formed.

Selection of meaning makes possible a myriad of cultures. Although we have never been to England, we can develop a love of, and identification with, the celebration of lessons and carols from King's College. Through annual television broadcasts it can become our Christmas tradition. At the same time the mass media culture retains some aspects of literate culture. We still focus on recording and storing knowledge (witness the archives of television stations and film companies), and we still pore over these recorded data in search of "true" meanings. As literate peoples engage written records in search of truth, we engage film footage of JFK's assassination to find out "what really happened." It is the details that make a difference. The answer, the knowledge, is out there somewhere in an objective record, which can be selected and interpreted.

The result of the combination of oral and literate cultures with the electronic communications culture is a mass media culture characterized by complex communications and meaning possibilities. We act through, react to and are influenced by mass media communications.

What is television's role in this culture? Speaking semiotically Robert Allen identifies television as a point of convergence for all the linguistic sign systems that give us meaning.[8] As Neil Postman puts it television has become our informer, our metaphor builder, the background for our lives, so that "all public understanding . . . is shaped by the biases of television." We are now into a second generation for whom television has been a member of the family, providing information, images and vision. We live in what Postman calls "the Age of Television."[9] Whatever we read as individuals, whatever conversations we take part in together, television often seems to frame our communication, link us and offer us common ground.

This became clear at a seminary faculty meeting, during which the faculty discussed possible names for a continuing education event at the school. In short order the name of a breakfast cereal, the title of a rock album, the title of a film, and a phrase from a recently televised movie were suggested (with varying degrees of seriousness). Television, in its capacities as advertiser, promoter, critic and entertainer framed our suggestions.

Thus, television is very much a part of the mass media cultural system that we identify as our way of life. Although it is not the sole communicator and does not replace other forms, it has centrality, both as a medium or form and as an institution that influences us.

RELIGIOUS EDUCATION
AS APPROACH TO TELEVISION CULTURE

Although there is no widespread agreement on a specific definition of the term "religious education" (a name given to the practice of education by and in the local church), a claim can be made for a broad vision of what the church undertakes in the education of its members. In general religious education is a ministry of the church which seeks to develop its members' knowledge, their ability to find meaning and reach understandings of what they encounter, and their ability to choose responses in their lives, church and world.

This broad goal is approached through helping persons gain information and concepts, the tools to understand these, and skill in applying what they know to their lives. The focus of this process may be on knowledge, meanings and practice of the church's faith tradition; on knowledge, meanings and responses to the world; or some combination that relates the faith tradition and world. While there is a broad range of programs and processes which different churches, persons and curricula may call "religious education," this general understanding can embrace the practices of most churches. In this understanding it is clear that education is a very human endeavor, related to a very human world. It is not a salvific or redemptive force, but a way the church engages and equips persons in relation to their world.

In light of this general concept of religious education, the questions to ask of the programs described at the beginning of this chapter are: How should Christians approach, view and react to television -- a popular, pervasive and widely consumed mass medium of our time? Is the form or medium itself good, bad or neutral? Is the culture framed by the system or institution of television good, bad or neutral?

In order to provide a framework and help sort through the variety of religious education programs focusing on television, this chapter employs a recasting of the heuristic typology found in H. Richard Niebuhr's *Christ and Culture*.[10] The Niebuhrian types are recast as:

I. Resistance: religious education that helps learners withdraw from or fight against the manifestations of television culture.

II. Adoption: religious education that embraces and uses television.

III. Preparation: religious education that accepts the presence of television and admits the learning it may enable, but focuses on developing the skills of "reading" the medium in order to make such culture learning possible.

IV. Critical Response: religious education that approaches television with a critical eye, enabling learners to discern and critique what is communicated in light of their religion.

V. Transformation: religious education that re-envisions what television can be.

TYPE I: RESISTANCE TO TELEVISION:
THE TELEVISION TURN-OFF

Marie Winn's latest television education effort is her classroom and family approach in *Unplugging the Plug-in Drug*. Winn is particularly concerned about television, both as a medium and as a cultural institution. For Winn it is not the content of television programs that is harmful or dangerous; it is the very existence of television in our midst that is wrong. Television is our culture: it becomes the way we exist as a group, it inculcates a particular vision, it teaches and favors certain values, it fills our time and space and is entirely oriented toward humans. For Winn television is clearly a dangerous social-control mechanism that exerts its sway over us. What is the danger in watching television? Ironically, television is a culture that dehumanizes its participants. Television culture, the environment made by humans in their own interest, actually works to destroy the very humanity of the persons it envelopes.[11]

Winn's concept of the *imago Dei* lies at the heart of her argument: to be created in the image of God is to have the capacity for relationship with God and other humans. To be human, as God intended, is to develop through relating, to be united by common experiences and bonds, and to grow through direct involvement with people. This is what it means to be a "community," and this communal nature is thwarted by television's very existence. It keeps people from being together in active ways. Television viewing becomes the substitute for doing things together.

Winn thoroughly agrees with Lewis Mumford's argument: the system of electronic communications technologies has altered our personalities, curtailing activity and experimentation in our lives, and replacing these essential human features with acquiescence to depersonalized "technics."[12] As Jacques Ellul suggests television is particularly guilty of this dehumanization. It gives the viewer everything as a powerful, consuming image, so the person's role is merely to "spectate" and absorb.[13] Winn's point is that this engrossing visual nature of television competes unbeatably with the human relational activities that are the essence of our human community. When the Ewings of "Dallas" can be your family, complete with money, crises, parties and romance, no mundane outside relationships are needed. The television family replaces the more prosaic persons we can relate to every day.

Corollary effects include: reduction of intellectual achievement (all that is required is consumption; Angela Lansbury will figure out the murderer by the end of the hour so we need only watch **her** mind work), reduction of physical fitness (armchair quarterbacks greatly outnumber quarterbacks on the playing field), reduction of personal inventiveness ("I don't know what to do, Mom." "Go watch TV."), reduction of learning (as active play is replaced with passive watching), and replacement of socialized living by immediate self-gratification (if you want to spend a week in Acapulco, just use American Express).[14] The result in Winn's view is that our culture, which is based on, permeated by and communicated by television, inhibits our very communal humanity. What was created as good is reduced and replaced by the culture. For Winn both the technology and the culture created are problems.

She responds by advocating withdrawal from the television culture around us, through a strategy called "television turn-offs." Her hope is to teach rejection of mass media culture by organizing television turn-offs based in school classrooms. A "Classroom Turn-Off" is a no-television experiment initiated by the teacher, using rituals and activities to make rejection of television a challenging learning adventure rather than a deprivation experience. The focus is on developing relational, growth-producing activities to replace television in the lives of learners. Through the process Winn hopes to bring about positive changes in the lives of the learners, to move them toward a fuller humanity as they withdraw from the dehumanizing contemporary television culture.

TYPE II: ADOPTION OF TELEVISION: TEACHING VIA MEDIA

At the opposite end of the spectrum from Winn lies a perspective that favors full participation in television culture. This approach relies heavily on the mass media communications theory of Marshall McLuhan to describe mass media culture as a positive development combining sight and sound in ways that fully involve the audience. As we see the images of the Welsh countryside in winter, hear the words read, catch the dialect and watch the characters interact, "A Child's Christmas in Wales" comes to life, and we are participants in community with all the aunts and uncles in a more complete way than when the words remain on the page.

The potential exists for television to increase our awareness of the whole world by increasing our exposure to a variety of people and places. The Vietnam War, called "the Living Room War" as it was broadcast into our homes with dinner each night, made a small country into a living and dying reality for Americans at their tables.

All the geography lessons and history books in the world could not accomplish what television did.

It is also possible for television to perform a kind of self-image validation by showing the viewer persons and problems similar to the viewer's life. Seeing someone "like you" portrayed on television can validate your identity. The presence of Jeri Jewell, a comedian with cerebral palsy, on "The Facts of Life," functions as positive affirmation of disabled young adults. The problem is that television has not fully lived up to these potentials, and true community is not formed. Absorption and control of the audience has dominated, while that audience has had no corresponding effect on television in return. Involvement is thus not complete, since there is no effective action on the viewer's part. Awareness of the world has not been fully achieved because control has landed in the hands of a small minority of economically powerful men. No one is seen or heard unless they have "market value." Identity validation has not been possible across the board in television. Only majority roles and situations are shown, so many identities are forgotten and denied.

Yet there is good news amid this situation. It is the **broadcast system** of television that is problematic, not the television medium itself. The communications medium has been tainted by the political-economic basis of our system, but the flaws in the communications system can be overcome by a turn to video. Like broadcast television, video is a totally involving medium, which can increase contact with various peoples and validate identities. Because control of the medium can rest in the hands of small groups who produce videos, and in the hands of viewers who determine their own viewing line-up, video can be used to empower groups or individuals and make personalized, contextualized communication possible.[15] Since video involves the whole person in the viewing experience, can be personalized, and is available for control by small marginalized groups, it follows that video is a form that can be fully developed by the church.

Tom Emswiler, for example, suggests a four-stage program of video use in religious education:

1. Use pre-recorded videotapes to present information on topics or issues. Here video simply communicates data to the receivers, offering the church educator a range of "expert sources" that may not be found within the church or community. For example, videos from the *Media Bible* might be used to present scripture stories, or the video series *Parenting Teenagers* from Group Books might be used in parent education.

2. Use pre-recorded videotapes to raise questions and ideas, then engage the video through sharing, based on prepared discussion guides. Churches can choose church-produced videos intended

for this purpose (as in the Presbyterian Church's *People of Faith and the Arms Race*, produced by PSCE Video Education Center. The video contains stopping points for discussion, questions and activities based around its central content). Or churches may use shows from commercial and public television, or theatrical films that raise pertinent questions.

3. Use interactive computer-video instruction pieces developed for study of particular units of content.

4. Produce your own videos in the church as part of a study. For example, a confirmation class might end its study of the meaning of "church" by producing their own video to present their images to the congregation.[16]

TYPE III: PREPARATION: TELEVISION LITERACY

For religious educators like Ronald Sarno, Marshall McLuhan's theories offer a starting point: electronic mass media are communication-enhancers. Media of any sort are not alien alterers of our being, imposed upon our nature (as Mumford would have it), but are simply extensions of one or more of our senses. Mass media do not replace our perceptions, but only increase our sensory abilities to perceive.[17] Television is one of the fullest, most complete media, extending and enhancing the presence and range of our senses. For example, the author had read, researched and taught about the dangers of nuclear war for ten years. She had a solid grasp of facts, figures, even effects of nuclear war. Yet, when she watched the television movie, *The Day After*, the horror became real in a more complete sense. She saw, heard, felt and feared. In McLuhan's terms that is the work of the television medium.

Sarno is aware of a danger in such media, however. It is always possible to become so totally absorbed by the medium that you are no longer aware or active in yourself. There is always a threat of becoming a totally passive receptor. When that happens the television medium is no longer an enhancer but has become a danger. To return to *The Day After*:the author was totally paralyzed by her fears following that movie. She could not see the strengths and weaknesses of the production, nor could she take any action in response to what she had seen. The medium had not drawn her in and aroused her to become a more active person, but had filled up a totally passive vessel.

For Sarno this total absorption in media is dangerous for theological reasons. Like Walter Ong he is concerned with the importance of God's communication with us. This communication does not come to us in a void, totally outside our lives and culture. God's Word comes to us **in** our culture. This is not to say that God's Word is identical with human culture, but that we receive it **in** our culture. God's Word is transcendent, not situationally determined, but it imparts to us the values that determine our lives **in** culture. To be Christian within our culture is to adhere to a Judeo-Christian value system, rooted in God's communication to us, bearing out these values in a cultural lifestyle.[18]

As Ong points out our Western culture is a mass media culture, so it is within that culture we receive, interpret and respond to God's communication.[19] For Sarno this means that we must become discerning media-consumers, able to "read" the images, structure and content of television.[20] Only when our senses are sharpened and used to the fullest can we hear, understand and respond to God in a mass media culture. Then we are participants in our cultural community, rather than mere products of it. "Media-literacy" is Sarno's term for this ability to "read" television in a way that fully engages the senses, promotes discernment of good from bad within the medium, and enables us to understand the medium's relationship to our faith.

It is important to note that Sarno is **not** critical of the existence, style, format or content of television per se, nor does he view religious education as criticism which lambasts television. Media-literacy is a technical form of television criticism aimed at understanding the content of the programs viewed, as New Criticism in literature is aimed at explication of texts.

For Sarno, although television is neither the source nor the judge of our values, it is our cultural medium and **can** be an enhancer of the lifestyle we develop in response to God. This enhancement is only possible, however, if we become media-literate, able to fully read and understand what we see and hear. Learners must become media-literate Christians who are able to discern in a television world, and this "literacy" training is the responsibility of religious education. Teachers and learners develop skill through viewing and discussing television programs, focusing not on the ideational content alone, but on **how** the medium communicates its message.

TYPE IV: CRITICAL RESPONSE TO TELEVISION: MEDIA-CONSCIOUSNESS

Neil Postman's thoughts on television have undergone a change over the past twenty years. In his most recent works he emerges as a strong critic of television as a cultural institution or system. Postman's argument begins with a basic assumption about communication, which is based on McLuhan's theory: the **form** of communication determines what can be communicated.[21] The medium of communication affects the content, the reception and what is done **with** the content. A communications medium is not merely a neutral vessel that can be filled with any meaningful content of choice. Any medium carries its own message and perspective, which shapes our way of thinking and the content of our culture.

As Postman sees it we are currently shaped by television, which frames our thinking and culture to fit an entertainment purpose. Our community, how we become part of it, and what it means to be part of it are all framed by the value of "being entertained." The medium of choice for us is television, a visual form of discourse created for and focused on entertaining us. Whatever content it communicates through visual images becomes entertainment. Concepts,

> **Our communications medium has recast Christianity itself as part of the entertainment.**

ideas, philosophies, arguments and details are communicated as trivialities, as the medium transforms them into a series of amusing images.[22] To be in community means to be entertained.

The problem with our dominant medium, then, is that it molds our culture into a homogeneity of entertainment, and so shapes our ways of thinking and viewing that we are unaware of how entertainment permeates all areas of our lives. We no longer think critically and seriously, but are determined by the amusing televised images. Recent presidential election campaigns are a case in point. Debates between the candidates are carefully constructed for their television value: the podiums are constructed to present each candidate at his best, the answers are limited to two minutes, the debaters are coached in how to connect with the television audience, and answers are rehearsed for maximum effect. Debate is no longer a matter of substantive discussion of issues, but a question of media image and personality.

Theologically Postman defines this general trivializing as sin, but he also carries his accusations even further into the heart of Christianity. Not only is our generally entertaining culture guilty of triviality. Our communications medium has recast Christianity itself as part of the entertainment. Christianity has moved into the television age by assimilating itself to the communications medium, and in so doing, it has been unavoidably transformed into trivial amusement. As television has shaped our world view, so it has reshaped Christianity. Postman makes his point in this description: Pat Robertson is the master of ceremonies of the highly successful "700 Club." He is modest, intelligent, and has the kind of charm television viewers would associate with a cool-headed talk show host. Indeed, he appears to use as his model of communication "Entertainment Tonight." His program includes interviews, singers and taped segments with entertainers. For example, all of the chorus girls in Don Ho's Hawaiian act are born-again.[23]

What hope is there for Christianity within this milieu? For Postman our only chance to regain diversity of thought forms and recover the essence of Christianity lies in developing "media-consciousness." Like Sarno, Postman wants us to be able to "read" the television medium, but his vision goes beyond Sarno's basically acceptant attitude.[24] Postman wants us to be aware of television as an entertainer, and thus neutralize its ability to transform all of our world into amusement. This is only possible if we understand **how** the medium shapes our thought and the content we communicate. We must not only become media-literate viewers, but must also be able to answer questions **about** the medium: What symbols of the world does television convey? What are the dominant symbolic forms that explain the world? From where does television draw its content? How and where do we experience television? To what extent is television influencing our knowledge and perceptions? How much of it are we exposed to, and how influenced are we?

Religious education must become a critical inquiry into the ways television shapes people's vision, faith and lives. It must raise questions about the medium and lead us to hold the pervasive television effects at bay.[25] Postman's religious education vision is **not** a Christ against culture rejection of mass media, but a call to become critically conscious Christians who can sort out media effects and respond, rather than being wholly determined by the media. For Postman this comprehensive explication of structures is media-consciousness. Only when this consciousness is achieved can there be hope of diversity and change.

TYPE V: THE NEED FOR ANOTHER APPROACH

The four religious education approaches described above represent the dominant ways the church teaches with and about television today. What can be said of these current approaches? Most religious education resources and strategies used in churches represent some wariness toward television. Television is seen primarily as an agent of social control, rather than an agent of change and diversity. While Marie Winn's television turn-off represents a drastic strategy that rejects both the medium and the institution, the more complex work of Postman agrees that the medium is an inherent entertaining controller. Even those who embrace the technology of the medium as an educational tool lean away from the institution of television in our culture, opting instead for a reworked video usage. Thus, most of the operating educational strategies advocate lessening the harm by replacing the media messages, or lobby for media-conscious education to counteract media effects. The system is suspect even when the form is embraced. While there is merit in what these approaches attempt, there is still a "step untaken." None of these approaches succeed in moving far beyond **reaction to** television's presence. They break little ground in suggesting ways the Christian community might transform the presence and influence of television.

What are the possibilities for transformative models of religious education in relation to television? Is it possible for television to become part of religious education in some other way? Are there transformational paradigms that actively redesign what television might be for and in the church? What might emerge if such work was undertaken? Several possibilities for exploration and development of transformational educational models emerge.

First, for those who find their Christian belief system rooted in an understanding of the Kingdom of God, elaborating a social responsibility theory that is grounded in Thomas Groome's theological concept of the Kingdom of God, and applying Groome's "shared praxis" methodology to media education could be attempted.[26]

> **"A complete religious education program may involve employment of all of the models described here. "**

If Postman is correct and television is basically an imagistic **story** medium, then it may have intrinsic value for the church in Groome's model. Groome's intent is to bring our present actions into dialogue with the Christian "story" and "vision." This story and vision may be well communicated by the imagistic television medium.

Second, those who find their faith expressed in the liberation theologies could pursue structural analysis to uncover the ideological tyranny of the broadcast media. Paulo Freire's conscientization pedagogy could then be explored in relation to media as an oppressor, focusing on recovering persons' control over their own lives, employing forms of television as one effective means.[27] Freire's work on "generative images" in people's lives, as the starting point for developing their control over their life's meaning and situation, may suggest that generative power lies in televised images for any culture. It would be possible to use these images as Freire uses pictures to help people gain control over their lives.

Third, those who find themselves drawn toward process theology, with emphasis on the ongoing transformation of our world and lives, could take note of Mary Elizabeth Moore's traditioning model of religious education[28] and develop that paradigm in relation to mass media. Content-centered media study would need to be developed, to bring intersections between the faith community and the media environment into focus. A phenomenological method of dialogue with the environment could emerge.

These three suggestions do not exhaust the possibilities, nor have any one of them been worked through far enough to display concrete examples. They are offered to the field of religious education at large as a challenge to develop a creative alternative to the current response types presently before us.

Finally, in light of this chapter's assumption that religious education is the church's mode of relating to and gaining critical perspective on culture, a complete religious education may involve employment of all of the models described here. In order to develop a deep, multi-dimensional understanding of television, of our television culture, of our engagement with television, and of our faith in relation to television, all five models are strategies worthy of use in every church. To engage television in religious education may be to encourage a television turn-off, to teach values through discussion of videos, to learn how to read television, to raise critical questions about the relationship between portrayals of the world on television and in our faith perspective, to become involved in media change, and to develop new ways of employing the medium. The religiously educated person may be one who is fluent in all these dimensions and can determine his or her own course.

KENNETH BEDELL

"When my first daughter was born our television broke, and it was years before we got it fixed. I think that's a sign that it's not an essential part of my life. At the time it broke there was a bar about a block away, and when there was something that I particularly wanted to watch, I would go down to the bar and watch it."

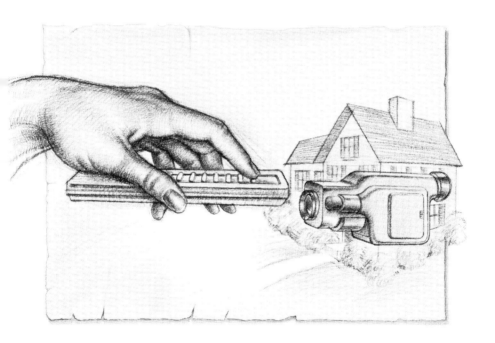

The television show that I find the most engaging is the 'Home Video Show.' It is democratizing television. It would be fun to figure out ways to bring television back around to the average person. It's a strange combination of really poorly done home videos with the glitz of high production values. For me the exciting thing about television is its potential for high production values and democracy.

"I watch television when it is possible to do a couple of things at once. Occasionally, like once a week, I watch it in order to be with my daughters. But I don't watch it for escape; I read for escape. Given a choice of doing other things, I generally choose to do something else rather than watch television. I don't see myself as part of the television generation.

"Most of the time when I watch television I use my critical faculties. Indeed, I upset my daughter because of my constant commentary. She says, 'You may watch with me as long as you don't talk about it.'"

"I find myself as a churchgoer very aware that there is no reference in church to what is happening on television. As a teacher I find myself thinking, 'Well, if I'm going to work on examples of things, I should try and pull things out of the television.' It's hard, though, when you don't see a lot of it. Other people are able to help. In my class the other day we were able to talk a little about Arsinio Hall and to use him in what we were doing. My students have television as their common experience. Frequently they don't have historical knowledge; they don't have theological knowledge; they don't have biblical knowledge. But they do know television."

"How does television affect my teaching? Probably we can't get a classroom's attention anymore for more than twelve or thirteen minutes. But I don't think about that question consciously."

"I don't know whether the church can sing on television or not. What television does with images and faces and presentations is superb. My daughter watches television better than I do. That's why I'm not ready to answer the question with a yes or no. My question still is, 'Does television make it either difficult or impossible for us to work out in our own culture or in our own time what is the gospel?'"

CHAPTER SIX

THE USE OF TELEVISION BY INTERPRETIVE COMMUNITIES

Kenneth Bedell

We all communicate. We take up a pen or speak into a telephone or move our fingers across a key board. In this way we share our feelings about the weather or our understanding of ultimate reality. We read posters on the wall, watch television or talk over the back fence. Communications seems simple to understand and master. It is the exchange of information which makes it possible for us to participate in human society. And we usually succeed in mastering the communications skills required to make it through the day.

But constantly we live in anxiety created by our confused communications. Communications between nations is a critical factor in insuring that a nuclear disaster does not occur. The "Hot Line" connecting Washington and Moscow symbolizes not only the importance of communications but its potential difficulties. The technology making it possible for two leaders in distant cities to send messages is quite easy to implement. But more than translators are needed at either end of the line to insure that there is clear communications. Do messages say what they appear to say? What is the hidden political message which needs to be understood? Even if one person has taken the trouble to learn the other's language, there are still deep cultural and social differences in meaning which can confuse communications.

Communication of religion presents its own unique problems. How can a faith be transmitted? What does it mean to communicate faith? Is that different from communicating information? Thomas Kuhn helped us see that even in science communications involves people accepting the authority of a particular community.[1] Especially the communication of religious faith depends upon the authority of particular communities. The issue we want to explore is the interrelation of religious communications and the authority of the interpretive community.

LEVELS OF COMMUNICATION

We can understand communications only when we recognize that there are different levels of communication. Every attempt to communicate involves at least three levels. These might be called literal, social relations and societal. When someone says to her daughter, "It is time for you to go to bed," she is communicating something on all three levels.

First, she is giving her daughter information about what time it is: it is 9:00 p.m. This is the literal interpretation of her communication. But secondly, she is communicating to her daughter, "I am your mother and have decided to exercise certain authority." This second message is understood just as clearly by her daughter as the first message. Sometimes she chooses to respond to the second level of communications by testing the limits of the mother's intention to exercise authority. In this case the daughter may make no move toward going to bed. On the first level she understood clearly the message. But she also understands that the mother is saying something about their relationship and she responds to that message. This second level of communications could be called the social relations dimension. The work of Erving Goffman exposed the importance of this level.[2] He studied asylums and observed responses to people with stigmas. His analysis of social interaction demonstrates the importance of this level.

The third is a more elusive level of social interaction in communications. It is the social structure which is defined by the choice of medium. Talking to a person requires some kind of physical presence. Although the mother may not think about options she has, the choice of medium through which to speak to her daughter carries with it a message of its own which is independent of either of the first two levels. This third level is by far the most subtle. As Neil Postman argues, "It is, I believe, a wise and particularly relevant supposition that the media of communication available to a culture are a dominant influence on the formation of the culture's intellectual and social preoccupations."[3]

THE MCLUHAN LEGACY

It was the genius of Marshall McLuhan to take the work of Harold Adams Innis and present an interpretation of modern media which recognized what is communicated by the very nature of the medium itself. McLuhan claimed that print or television communicate particular meanings which are determined by the nature of the medium.[4] We have found that sometimes there is a reaction in the classroom to McLuhan's slogan "The medium is the message." The common response is: "How can you say that the medium itself is the message when a medium like television can be used to present religion or to deliver pornography?" Students find it difficult to give up the idea that communications media are not neutral in relation to what they communicate.

The debate is naturally tied to the debate about the social neutrality of all technology. Langdon Winner's book, *Autonomous*

Technology, is an examination of attitudes toward technology. He argues that an initial neutrality is lost once the technology is in place.

> At the outset, the development of all technologies reflects the highest attributes of human intelligence, inventiveness, and concern. But beyond a certain point, the point at which the efficacy of the technology becomes evident, these qualities begin to have less and less influence upon the final outcome; intelligence, inventiveness, and concern effectively cease to have any real impact on the ways in which technology shapes the world.[5]

When we present Winner's arguments to students we find them unconvinced. They respond that it may be that certain technologies such as atomic weapons have modified the nature of relations between nations of the world, but people could decide how to use or dispose of nuclear weapons. Just as it is not the weapons themselves which determine international relations, so technology does not determine the meanings of communications.

❝You cannot use smoke signals to do philosophy. Its form excludes the content. ❞

Students usually argue for the "tool-use concept of technology." As Winner explains, this concept, "essentially unchanged since Francis Bacon, was universally accepted as an accurate model of all technical conduct. All one had to do was to see that the tools were in good hands."[6] Students argue that the issue of communications is not the nature of the communications tool but the nature of the people who are using the specific tool. Their reasoning: Why can't I take television or radio or printed books and use them to communicate any message which I wish to communicate?

Why do we hold so tightly to the idea that communications media are neutral tools which we can use for good or evil? One reason may be that as a part of our everyday experience we encounter a variety of media being used for many different communications purposes. Beyond that we sense our own power to use media. We actually use a written message or the telephone to transmit our own ideas. We feel in control of those messages. Even in the example of the discussion between the mother and her daughter about bedtime, it appears that the second level of communications is readily accessible. She could have a discussion with her daughter about their relationship, and they could come to a mutually agreeable arrangement about her bedtime. At this level McLuhan's idea does not seem to fit with every day experience.

Joshua Meyrowitz' sophisticated reworking of McLuhan's ideas is more plausible. Meyrowitz argues that "the structure of a society's social roles is susceptible to change as a result of shifts in the use of media of communications."[7] But to say that the structure of a society's social roles is susceptible to change appears to beg the question for those who argue that all forms of media are culturally neutral and are simply a way of passing a message from one person to another. Yet Meyrowitz points the way to more clearly understand the relationship between society and communications. While a particular communications technology does not **determine** the structure of a society's social roles, each technology presents its own limits, which can be exploited or not exploited.

Neil Postman illustrates the foundation for this argument by talking about the use of smoke signals by Native Americans. He points out that smoke signals are an interesting technological development which provided a means of communications over distance. But it is important to recognize that smoke signals are not an appropriate technology for discussing philosophical arguments.

> Puffs of smoke are insufficiently complex to express ideas on the nature of existence, and even if they were not, a Cherokee philosopher would run short of either wood or blankets long before he reached his second axiom. You cannot use smoke signals to do philosophy. Its form excludes the content.[8]

The same story can be told in a book or a movie, but it cannot be told in exactly the same way using the different media. This concept, of course, is not new. Plato recognized the impact which writing would have on his culture and celebrated the shift from oral-based study to writing-based study.

Beginning with the recognition that each communications technology carries with it particular possibilities and limits, we can move beyond McLuhan's oversimplification. As Meyrowitz argues it is not that a new technology causes changes in social relations. Rather, new communications technologies carry with them a potential for new social relations. The reason that McLuhan is able to make a credible argument for the power of media to influence the direction of society is that historically we can discern that there are social changes which accompany the adoption of new forms of communications technology. It is quite easy in retrospect to see how these new social relations are related to the potential inherent in the new technologies.

Television provides an excellent example of a medium of communications which was appropriated in a particular way that resulted in redefinitions of social relationships. Meyrowitz claims that television has "tended to merge many formerly distinct social situations, blur the dividing line between private and public behaviors, and tear apart the once taken-for-granted bond between physical position and social 'position.'"[9] However, from these observations it does not follow that the new technologies have determined the changed social relations. We are still left with the question of whether new communications technologies simply provide new possibilities or whether they determine patterns of social interaction. Is Postman correct when he claims, "Marx understood well that the press was not merely a machine but a structure for discourse, which both rules out and insists upon certain kinds of content and inevitably, a certain kind of audience"?[10]

David Noble's careful study of the relationship between technology and changing social relations is helpful at this point. His study of the computerization of the machine shop floor concluded:

> The managerial quest for control, which was coupled with a corresponding desire to reduce the control exercised by workers and their unions, was less a means to other ends -- such as efficiency and profit -- than an end in itself: the enlargement of authority, the securing of positions and prerogatives of power, the defense and assertion of managerial decision-making "rights."[11]

The point is that technology does not just appear with its related social implications. Technology is appropriated and used as society makes necessary adaptation. With communications technology as with all technology the ultimate role which it plays in society is the result of a complicated adjustment in the social relations which surround the introduction and use of the technology. And these adjustments are made in relationship to the existing interests and powers in a given society. This is the reason that Meyrowitz uses the word "may" when he outlines "the 'mechanism,' or process, through which changes in media may change social behavior."[12] It is not that media cause social change or determine the nature of that social change. But media may play an important part in the social changes. The impact of adopting new technologies is not always (usually it is not) recognized before dramatic social changes have occurred.

Neil Smelser's study of the industrialization of England demonstrates the complicated relationship between the adoption of new technologies and the social relationships which are modified surrounding the new technologies.[13] He reports that the industrialists at first allowed the family authority structure to move into the factories. The movement to end child labor was ultimately successful because capitalists began to see that as long as parents brought their children to work in the factories it would be impossible to gain complete control over the work force. Only when the authority of the parent was removed from the factory could the capitalist be in complete control. The adoption of the new technologies of industrialization were accompanied by far reaching efforts to modify the social relationships between parents and children. In this case both the adoption of new technology and the related social changes have roots in the larger struggle in the society involving the reorganization of social relations that accompanied capitalism.

If communications technologies appear to has a neutrality, and if historically the adoption of new technologies have resulted in reorganization of some social relations, and if the adoption of new technologies appears to be a complicated process related to various forces in a given society, then how are we to interpret the influence and place of communications technology? Is there any way to predict the impact which new communications technology will have? Is there actually a third level of communications which is the communication of the particular medium which we choose to use? Having examined the ideas which surround the McLuhan thesis in a new light, we return to a further consideration of the three levels of communication.

AUTHORITY OF INTERPRETIVE COMMUNITIES

Stanley Fish has suggested a method of understanding communications which makes it possible to apply the McLuhan thesis in a way which meets the objections of persons who do not accept a media determinism. Fish is not primarily concerned with the question of communications. Like McLuhan and Postman he is a professor of English. He is searching for an acceptable method of interpreting literature. Fish argues that "sentences emerge only in situations, and within those situations, the normative meaning of an utterance will always be obvious or at least accessible, although within another situation that same utterance, no longer the same, will have another normative meaning that will be no less obvious and accessible."[14] The meaning is determined by "the authority of interpretive communities." People will agree with the interpretation of a communication when they share a common interpretive community. This does not mean that two people reading the same sentence will interpret it in exactly the same way. But if they share a common interpretive community, they will be able to talk about the meaning of the sentence and come to a consensus or an understanding of their differences.

According to Fish the "identification of context and the making of sense" occur simultaneously. He argues, "To be in a situation is to see the words, these or any other, as already meaningful." He recognizes that "being in a situation" requires previous experience which places us in the situation. In describing a particular event in which a colleague first misunderstood a question and then recognized what the question meant, Fish says, "How, then, did he do it? In part, he did it because he **could** do it; he was able to get to this context because it was already part of his repertoire for organizing the world and its events."[15]

There are certainly situations in which we hear a sentence but we cannot identify the context because our past experience does not make this part of our repertoire for organizing the world and its events. In this case it is necessary to step outside the sentence itself to learn the context. No amount of study or examination of the sentence will reveal its meaning. Fish raises the question of how one can discover the meaning of a sentence when the context is unavailable. He says that it

> does not mean one is trapped forever in the categories of understanding at one's disposal (or the categories at whose disposal one is), but that the introduction of new categories or the expansion of old ones to include new (and therefore newly seen data) must always come from the outside or from what is perceived, for a time, to be the outside.[16]

If two people are going to communicate, then it is necessary for them to begin at a point where there is an agreement about what is reasonable to say so that "a new and wider basis for agreement could be fashioned." Fish concludes,

> meanings come already calculated, not because of norms embedded in the language but because language is always perceived, from the very first, within a structure of norms. That structure, however, is not abstract and independent but social. Therefore it is not a single structure with a privileged relationship to the process of communication as it occurs in any situation, with its assumed background of practices, purposes, and goals.[17]

This understanding of meaning is consistent with the arguments Peter Berger and Thomas Luckmann present in their book, *The Social Construction of Reality*. They argue,

> Primary socialization ends when the concept of the generalized other (and all that goes with it) has been established in the consciousness of the individual. At this point he is an effective member of society and in subjective possession of a self and a world. But this internalization of society, identity and reality is not a matter of once and for all. Socialization is never total and never finished.[18]

Fish concludes that "all objects are made and not found, and that they are made by the interpretive strategies we set in motion." We participate in institutions which precede us and which we can inhabit. "We have access to the public and conventional senses they make." These institutions are not only available to the person who receives a message or communication. Communication occurs when there is a shared interpretive community. According to Fish membership in these communities is continually changing. "It changes laterally as one moves from subcommunity to subcommunity, and it changes through time once interdicted interpretive strategies are admitted into the ranks of the acceptable."[19] The interpretive communities make it possible for us to identify the first level of communications which we have called literal. It is our participation in an interpretive community which makes it possible for us to discern literal meaning.

But the social relations and societal levels of communications are also based upon interpretive communities. These two levels are at times hidden from us. We can only see them when perceptive observers such as Meyrowitz or Postman point them out to us. We are also less likely to consciously participate in the establishment of the authority of these communities. These are the more basic power struggles within a society between groups and interests. Yet the establishment of these authority structures are the product of human invention. That is why students have an intuition that the use of particular media does not determine the message it delivers. Rather the message is constructed out of the use of the media. This use is a social product. It grows out of a variety of power struggles within the society.

IMPLICATIONS FOR THE CHURCH

For the most part the church is the recipient of the possibilities for interpretation. The church is a minor player in the determination of any of the issues which are central to the establishment of authoritative interpretive communities in the society as a whole. Only in the areas which are specific to ·   icipation in the church does the church establish its own authoritative interpretive community.

The importance of authoritative communities for the establishment of meaning can be seen in the conflict in the church over control of how the Bible will be read and understood. The distinctions between liberals and fundamentalists illustrate the diversity of opinion between interpretive communities. For fundamentalists and other literalists there is no crisis. At both the literal, personal relations and at the societal levels, biblical interpretation is structured. The fundamentalist interpretation of scripture is within a context of accepting the authority of the preacher. Following the framework proposed by Fish we can see fundamentalists as intentionally formulating a tight interpretive community.

The liberals have a much more difficult problem. They desire to use the best and most generally acceptable critical tools available to understand the scriptures. Without embarrassment liberals want to use literary and form criticism, along with historical analysis, to assist them with the interpretation of the Bible. By deciding to accept the societal assumptions of the predominant interpretive community, they are presented all the same problems which the society at large faces. A crisis is caused by the loss of an authoritative interpretive community.

George Barna and William Paul McKay's analysis of the reasons people respond to fundamentalist religion illustrates the key role of the community of interpretation. Liberal denominations will continue to decline and independent churches will grow.

> This probability is consistent with other expected shifts in the lifestyles of Christians: the preference for participatory forms of government; the quest for personalization in the work place; increasing involvement in individual sports at the expense of team sports; more favorable attitudes toward small companies; the continued preference for a nonurban environment; and the like. These are expressions of freedom and individuality. Worshipping at a church that is not tied to a distant, impersonal, hierarchical authority structure complements those expectations.[20]

Barna and McKay are typical of authors supporting the fundamentalist approach to religion who recognize that individuality and the apparent absence of authoritative structures attract people to fundamentalism.

PRESENT CRISES

The problem of community in modern society has been recognized for a long time. John Dewey's 1927 book, *The Public and Its Problems*, pointed to the predicament. He wrote, "The Great Society created by steam and electricity may be a society, but it is not community. The invasion of community by the new and relatively impersonal and mechanical modes of combined human behavior is the outstanding fact of modern life."[21] Dewey argued that "to learn to be human is to develop through the give-and-take of communication an effective sense of being an individually distinctive member of a community; one who understands and appreciates its belief, desires and methods, and who contributes to a further conversion of organic powers into human resources and values."[22]

Dewey wrote long before the invention of television but he sounds surprisingly like Meyrowitz who argues that American society has been modified by electronic media. Meyrowitz describes the destruction of specific communities and the merging of others. "By merging discrete communities of discourse, television has made nearly every topic and issue a valid subject of interest and concern for virtually every member of the public."[23] But in the process television has limited the concerns and interests to entertainment. As Postman argues, "Entertainment is the supra-ideology of all discourse on television. No matter what is depicted or from what view, the overarching presumption is that it is there for our amusement and pleasure."[24]

To put this in another way the societal level of communications through electronic media is that there is no community. Each individual receives the electronic message which is designed to entertain and to please. The television producers compete to generate larger and larger audiences. The information conveyed by television has lost its societal meaning. The message is sent out to everyone without providing a clear social context within which it can be understood. Political conventions are no longer occasions for determining the political futures of political parties. Rather they are staged to entertain television audiences. The relationship between political leaders and citizens has become one of entertainer and entertained.

When the dominant medium of communications at the societal level communicates that there is no community, and that same medium is based on the assumption that communications can be supplanted by entertainment that does not assume a human interaction component, then there is a crisis in communications. The crisis is caused by the fact that although electronic media appear to serve the function of communications and to replace print as the primary medium of communications, the electronic medium as it has developed has undercut the social relations and societal basis for communications by denying the place of community in communications. While years are spent teaching children how to read and how to understand what they read, infants are placed in front of television screens. Only the television itself teaches them how to understand what they see. As these children grow older there is no reason for them to suspect communications is anything more than entertainment.

These crises in communications are related to the development of mass culture. Stuart Ewen and Elizabeth Ewen point out that "[m]ass culture is for those who have become masses. The viability of a capitalist mass culture is predicated on the assumption that all others -- other than ourselves -- are strangers." The result is narcissism or individualism. But this narcissism presents a problem.

> Precisely as capitalism's rise has meant the decline of many of the customary bonds of mutual dependency, it has erected and elevated new systems of unification and dependence: systems of communication and transport; agencies of mass production and mass impression....The goal of the advertising industry is to link the isolated experience of the spectator with the collectivized impulses and priorities of the corporation. The contingencies of the self will be thwarted by the unity of the commodity and the facts of the marketplace. In the commodity lies a newly realized self, the promise of community.[25]

But there is only the promise of community. The problems which Dewey saw in the relationship between the individual focus of modern society and the development of community are not overcome when everyone shares in wearing the same clothing or watching the same television program. The societal message of electronic media is that there is no community.

John B. Thompson has suggested that

> it is not so much unification and homogenization, but rather fragmentation and differentiation, which may be responsible for the social cohesion that exists in Western liberal democracies. Perhaps the principal division in this regard is the insulation of the economy and the polity, which prevents questions of industrial organization from appearing as political issues.[26]

At first Thompson's argument contradicts Meyrowitz' suggestion that electronic media tend to merge social distinctions. But Thompson is pointing to the result of making social distinctions insignificant. With electronic media the social context of what we see is lost. So it is natural that the connection between industrial organization and politics is also lost. Actually mass media makes it possible for this separation. In describing Claude Lefort's analysis of ideology, Thompson says,

> The new ideology depends crucially on the mass media, by means of which the implicit homogenization of the social field is achieved. The broadcasting of debates and discussions dealing with all aspects of life, from science and politics to art, cookery and sex, creates the impression that the social relation is fully reciprocal, that speech circulates without internal obstacles and constraints. The word of the expert appears as anonymous and neutral, expressing and diffusing objective knowledge; but at the same time it singularizes itself, assumes the attributes of the person in order to reach an audience which, in spite of its mass and dispersion, is brought together by the very proximity and familiarity of the one who speaks. The most banal programmes on radio and television, the chat shows and question times, become inner sanctums in a mass society, intimate worlds where the sense of distance and adversity has been abolished. Therein lies the imaginary dimension of communication; it proves the constant assurance of the social bond, attests to the permanent presence of the 'between-us' (entrenous), and thereby effaces the intolerable fact of social division.[27]

HOW DID WE GET HERE?

We are still left with the question of why was television ever invented or after its invention why was it appropriated by society? Our recognition that John Dewey pointed to problems of community and individualism long before television demonstrates that it makes no sense to say that the problem of the development of community in modern society has only developed since television has become the dominant medium of communication.

Lewis Mumford's *Technics and Civilization* meticulously presents the history of events which led to the invention and adoption of the machines necessary for the industrial revolution. He points to the cultural preparation which made it possible not only for technologies to be invented, but also for them to find a supportive setting in which they could develop.[28]

Mumford focuses on the clock, which was one of the first machines of the industrial age. It was an expression of the values of time keeping which developed in monastic communities in the years preceding the fourteenth century. Scholastic theology with its systematic approach to spiritual matters helped pave the way for those who would design machines which acted in completely predictable and repeatable ways. The printing press was one of the first practical applications of the developing machine age. The printing press was also an expression of the values growing out of the monasteries where meticulous reproduction of scriptures was highly valued.

> **Electronic media developed in a setting in which individualism and narcissism had already become the dominant values.**

The fact that Luther's translation of the Bible was one of the very first materials produced by a printing press is a demonstration that the machine age and the printing press were an outgrowth of attempts to express the most basic values of the society in which machines were developed.

To observe as McLuhan and others do that the printing press transformed the nature of social relations and resulted in a redefinition of basic values in society is to overlook the fact that clocks, machines and the printing press were themselves only possible at a certain point in the development of social values. Machines were adopted by a society which was conditioned by an understanding of God which was mechanical. Thomas Aquinas in his *Summa Theologica* culminated the development of theology in this direction with a description of exactly how God works and what can be expected of God. As Mumford points out the machine age was also preceded by an end of animism. This made it possible for material objects to take on a mechanical predictability so that a document prepared by a machine was of as much value as a document carefully copied by a human hand. The point is that printing presses did not simply stumble into existence so that they could forever change the structure of society. The printing press was quickly appropriated by society because it was an expression of the most profound values of the society. In this case the values were that ultimate reality is predictable and reproducible. This reflected the God of the scholastic theologians and the culture which preceded the invention of the printing press.

In the same way television was not an accident or simply the result of universities producing clever engineers and scientists. There was a cultural preparation for the particular way that television has been appropriated by society. That cultural preparation can be seen in the destruction of community which Dewey lamented. Electronic media developed in a setting in which individualism and narcissism had already become the dominant values. In this case it was the success of Martin Luther's theology and the predominant theological understanding of ultimate reality of the Reformation. Thomas Aquinas' theology based on meticulously following the known rules of how God works was replaced by a theology that taught that each individual is responsible for developing an individual and personal relationship with God. This new theology was sometimes separated from its roots in the church, but individualism became the basis of the dominant value system. Out of the dominant value system of the twentieth century came electronic media. Once in place the electronic media did exactly what it was designed to do. Electronic media became the ultimate tool in destroying community while providing a vehicle for the support of individualism in a mass society. Electronic media has not caused a crisis. Rather they are an expression of the values of individualism.

WHAT CAN THE CHURCH DO?

Electronic media have not had sufficient time to demonstrate fully their own logic. Up to this point they have been guided by the forces which brought them into existence. The same was true for the early years of the printing press. At first the printing press only increased the number of manuscripts which were available. It was only later that the availability of large numbers of printed documents began to modify the social structure.

The audience which a minister faces from the pulpit on Sunday morning is a group of people formed by the assumptions of electronic media. They assume that information can be delivered to them without a social context or without what Meyrowitz calls a "place." The audience is also influenced by the diversity to which Thompson points. There is an assumption that whatever happens in church should have value only for its own sake. But what happens at church is not connected to what happens at work or in politics.

The interest in making a clear distinction between church and society has a long history which is related to the destruction of community and the celebration of the individual. The development of mass culture and electronic communications has undercut even more the liberal church's position on these matters. In the church and society debates we can see an arena where loss of a sense of participation in community has created an audience for the churches which makes religion and politics into unrelated opportunities to be entertained.

The criterion of entertainment is not left at the door of the church when people enter. The primary criterion that people coming to church have to judge what they experience there is whether it is entertaining. In the fundamentalist churches great effort is expended to create a very specific community of interpretation which is described as being at odds with the primary cultural values. The claim that the authoritative interpretive community of fundamentalist churches is in opposition to the dominant culture may not be true, but there is a clear distinction between the fundamentalists who attempt to define a distinct community of interpretation and the liberals who attempt to adopt the dominant cultural understandings which undercut an authoritative community of interpretation.

At this point the electronic media are still under the influence of the values which brought them into existence. The appearance of the printing press was accompanied by Martin Luther's response to scholastic theology. To date there has been no comparable voice raising objections or presenting alternatives to the value system of individualism. For the church the result is that, so far, the only strategy is to attempt to compete in a fragmented world for an audience. Thus the minister sees himself or herself on Sunday morning as being in competition with a variety of alternative entertainments. This situation is the result of adopting the strategy of liberalism at a time when the society is moving into a communications crisis which is resulting from the adoption of electronic media.

We draw two conclusions from these observations. First, church leaders need to take seriously the importance of discovering and articulating ultimate values in an electronic culture which does not seem interested in such a quest. Second, church leaders need to look carefully at how electronic media could be used in ways that are consistent with the values which they espouse.

The first conclusion assumes that this is the time for theologians and pastors to examine more carefully the theology which focuses on the individual response to God. A theology of the role of the authoritative interpretive community in our knowledge of and relation to God is needed, such as we find in the theology of George Lindbeck and Stanley Hauerwas. Just as Luther proposed radical new ways of understanding the Christian message, so this is the time for a radical look at God in a media culture. We need to ask the question again, what exactly is God and what is of ultimate importance in a television culture?

The second conclusion assumes that there are alternative ways to use electronic media which do not have the same devastating effects as those described by Meyrowitz and Postman. While electronic media may have built in constraints in the way they can be used, there are certainly alternative ways of using them. For example, Dennis Benson's experiments with the development of interactive videos illustrate that Christians can look for alternative ways to use communications technology. Interactive videos make no sense when they are viewed alone. They must be used in a setting where a group of people first watch a section of video and then turn the video off and talk to each other. The video serves as a stimulus for interaction and underscores a theology of the church and of Christian existence within an interpretive community. There are many other ways that the church can experiment with ways to use electronic technology.

Our suspicion is that the key to finding a way thorough our new electronic media culture is to rediscover the church as a distinctive community. The church needs to be intentional about developing communities which are not merely reflections of the communities of interpretation in the larger society. These communities will require commitment on the part of individuals who will discover with each other, not only an understanding of ultimate reality and primary values, but also, ways that the technologies of communications available in this age can be used to bring more people into the authoritative interpretive community of meaning which they discover.

NORMAN E. THOMAS

"I had fifteen years in Africa with no television. We raised our children with no television. We came back with two pre-teenagers, and their first question was, 'Why don't we own a television set?' Soon they were spending all their time with the neighbor's children. We figured we'd better buy a set."

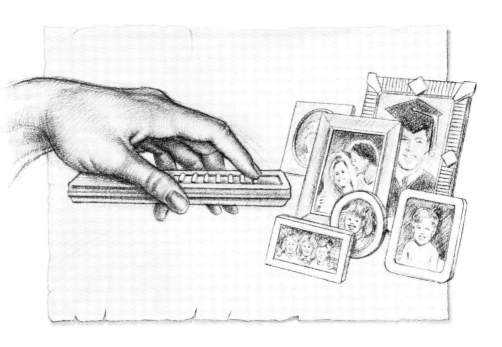

❝ *I'd like to produce on television the living biographies of common ordinary people and how they incarnated the faith in their lives. I'd try to build a bridge of personal understanding, some empathy for persons of other cultures, particularly the disadvantaged.* **❞**

"We had to deal with these children who had been raised in Africa, in a culture in which violence is not part of the play of children. Only when you have lived in that type of culture and come back to this one do you realize how pervasive violence is on American television, not only how many murders you see on television, but also the play and toys that the children have."

"What was striking to me about the 1989 Oscar awards in January was that the show was beamed to a world audience for the first time. A billion people saw it. Think of the exposure to other peoples, other cultures, as well as of course to the market of U.S. culture. Television provides the possibility of really getting a side of, if not inside, another culture and the feelings of people in another place. The revolutions that occurred in Eastern Europe and South Africa took place in part because the media were present and able to beam what happened there to us and was able to receive our response as well. There is now the opportunity to think of people as a world family and a world community in ways that were not as present before. A true participatory community is now possible. That's what makes the Eastern Europe revolution 'great'--the participation in it."

"When I grew up as a boy *National Geographic* introduced me to other cultures. The potential for television is using more of the senses than just visual. Of course the issue of who controls the medium is critical, and that is what I bring out in my chapter. This is a real concern for persons in communications leadership internationally, like the World Council of Churches. Who is going to control the images, and is it going to be centralized control in which the possibility of an international community is strangled? With the growing gap between the haves and have-nots, are the latter going to have any participation in what is programmed?"

"As I view television critically in the areas where I have inside knowledge, like Zimbabwe and Nicaragua, and as I watch '60 Minutes'-type documentaries about other parts of the world I know by inside information, I become intensely dissatisfied with the coverage. This gives me a profound dis-ease."

CHAPTER SEVEN

TELEVISION AND THE CHURCH'S GLOBAL MISSION

Norman E. Thomas

In the New York office of RAVEMCCO, the religious media commission, there is displayed a photograph which has caught the attention of many visitors. It shows a Filipino farmer preparing his field with a buffalo and steel-tipped plow, a method of planting from the Iron Age. On one horn of the buffalo, however, is a transistor radio.[1]

The church's global mission is deeply affected by the communications revolution which that picture symbolizes. From the days of Matteo Ricci, the pioneer Jesuit missionary to China who repaired the emperor's clocks while proclaiming the gospel, missions from the West to what we now call the two-thirds world of Africa, Asia, Latin America and Oceania have been known for their simultaneous espousal of the gospel and technology. David Livingstone sought to end the slave trade in Africa through the introduction of "Commerce, Civilization and Christianity." The first radios heard, or airplanes seen, by many peoples of Africa and Latin America were those of the missionaries.

What is the significance today of the electronic media for the church's mission? Is there congruence or incongruity between the presuppositions, theology and methodologies of persons in mission and leaders in the electronic media?

There is no simple answer to these questions. In this chapter we shall explore both congruences and dissonances between contemporary mission (in both action and reflection) and the electronic media. On the one hand both emphasize experiential learning. Furthermore, both favor receptor-oriented communication. On the other hand television tends to be controlled by a few, thereby enhancing imperialistic rather than democratic forms of communication. Issues of just distribution and just control must be raised. Finally, we shall consider models of person-centered communications which have contributed already to the renewal of churches in many countries and continents through base communities and interactive television.

EXPERIENTIAL KNOWING

In 1969 the prestigious *International Review of Missions* dropped the final "s" in its name. This signaled a fundamental shift in theology and praxis for the world missionary movement. Previously the emphasis had been on "saving souls" or on "building the church," with the great commission of Jesus as the mandate. The new emphasis in mission theology was on God's saving action in the total human world, with mission redefined as "the total responsibility of the church for the world."[2] Increasingly Jesus' Nazareth sermon in Luke 4:16-21 was accepted as a mandate alongside Matthew 28:19-20.

Simultaneous with this shift in mission theology, a shift in global Christianity took place. While many first and second world churches in western and eastern Europe were in decline in membership, participation and influence in the 1945-1985 period, Christianity grew rapidly in the two-thirds world of Africa, Asia, Latin America and Oceania. By 1985, for the first time since the apostolic age, the majority of Christians were to be found on those continents. Their leadership in world ecumenical and confessional bodies influenced the shift in mission theology.

❝Liberation theologians... provide an epistemology which opens the church both to its mission and to the acceptance of new technologies such as those of the electronic media.❞

Since the mid-'60s the most significant theological development in the two-thirds world, if not globally, has been the rise of liberation theologies. Liberation theologians share with other theologians the understanding that theology is critical reflection about Christian faith and witness. They differ in their method in which they begin with persons in action in concrete situations. "Liberation theology begins with concrete experience of the faith as a liberation praxis," asserts Raul Vidales. The path of reflection begins with faith as a lived reality. Right from the outset there exists a dialectic interplay between "ongoing concrete history and incarnation of the divine message."[3] From this perspective theology begins with knowledge of God in action.

This epistemology has firm biblical antecedents. When the disciples of John the Baptist, concerned with ideas, came to Jesus saying, "Are you he who is to come, or shall we look for another?" Jesus did not answer with a creedal formula. Although the invitation was there to confine theology to the realm of ideas, Jesus chose another way: Go and tell John what you **hear** and **see:** the blind receive their sight and the lame walk, lepers are cleansed and the deaf hear, the dead are raised up, and the poor have good news preached to them (Mt 11:2-6). The Christ was to be known not through an abstract formula but through experiencing agape love in concrete action.

Juan Luis Segundo finds it necessary in liberation theology to interpret the word of God as it is addressed to us here and now. It is the compulsion "at every step to combine the disciplines that open up the past with the disciplines that help to explain the present" that distinguishes the liberation theologian from the traditional academic theologian. Segundo terms his special methodology the "**hermeneutic circle.**" For such a circle there are two preconditions. First, persons have profound and enriching questions and are suspicious about their real situation. Second, they discover a new interpretation of the Bible that is equally profound and enriching.

Segundo gives four "factors" in the circle. First is the way of experiencing reality which leads to "ideological suspicion." There follows a reflection on experience which relates to one's entire world view and one's theology in particular. A third factor relates both experience and theological reflection to biblical interpretation, often with a resulting "exegetical suspicion." Finally, there results a new hermeneutic or way of interpreting the faith with which the person goes on to experience a new reality as the hermeneutical circle begins again.[4]

"Is theology a deductive science," Luis G. del Valle asks, "a science of principles from which conclusions are drawn and which also uses principles or conclusions from other sciences? Or is it a science akin to the empirical sciences, a science that takes in data that must then be subjected to verification through hypotheses and is therefore modified in the process of becoming known?" His answer is that "on the **epistemological** level, we will treat theology more as an empirical science."[5] Jose Miguez Bonino agrees, arguing that there is no truth outside or beyond the concrete historical events in which persons are involved as agents. But he insists that such a theological epistemology does not minimize the historical revelation in Jesus Christ, which is "not an abstract theoretical knowledge but a concrete existence: the existence in love."[6]

That theology begins in action is a common premise of liberation theologians on every continent. Those attending an influential 1983 consultation of third world theologians declared: "Theology partakes of the rhythm of action, contemplation, worship, and analysis that marks the life of the people of God." The fundamental subject of theology for them was not abstract understandings of God, but rather "the restless presence of God in the history and culture of the oppressed."[7]

This "epistemological break" in liberation theology has an affinity to the communications theory of Marshall McLuhan, whose contention that "the medium is the message" continues to confound traditionalists. McLuhan contended that the "electronic implosion," which makes of our globe no more than a village, has heightened our human awareness of responsibility to an intense degree.

Critical information is no longer controlled by a power elite in an electronically configured society. Instead it potentially is available to all at the same time. "The mark of our time," McLuhan says, "is its revulsion against imposed patterns. We are suddenly eager to have things and people declare their beings totally."[8] The result, he believes, is an aspiration for wholeness, empathy and depth of awareness.

McLuhan contrasted the psychic effect of the printed word and the television image. The printed book intensified the fixed point of view, detachment and non-involvement, "the power to act without reacting." The television image, by contrast, is ever-changing yet induces a higher degree of audience involvement. Thus in both liberation theology and in television, an "epistemological break" occurs. And in both an inclusive, participatory and experiential approach to knowing is affirmed.

Where McLuhan and liberation theologians differ, however, is on issues of personal freedom and responsibility. McLuhan believed that the "epistemological break" was determined by the new technology. Hugo Assmann, a prominent Latin American theologian, presents an alternative perspective. On the one hand he admits that those who control the mass media influence powerfully the formal flow of information and value formation. On the other hand he argues that the poor have alternative means of communication among themselves and with society.[9] Both the communicator and the receptor have power as well as freedom of choice. Media can lead to enlightened thought and action instead of unreflective passivity.

In 1983 church communicators from Latin America and the Caribbean considered the methodology for reflection and practice of Christian communications. No longer did they wish to start with rational theological discourse. Instead they preferred to identify with "the concrete situation of Christians who are often alienated and treated *en masse*" by those who limit themselves to a wordy and authoritarian transmission of the gospel message. They concluded that "only through this praxis can theological knowledge be generated which will clarify and enlighten the process of communication."[10] An analogy may be found in the experience of two of Jesus' disciples on the road to Emmaus (Lk 24:13-35). They were confined in an epistemological box. Their categories of thought were traditional. They assumed that insight came only through intellectual discourse. They were not open to a knowing of God through other types of experience. But an epistemological break took place as the risen Christ took bread and broke it and gave it to them "and their eyes were opened." It is such openness to praxis-learning that characterizes liberation theologians at their best. They provide an epistemology which opens the church both to its mission and to the acceptance of new technologies such as those of the electronic media.

RECEPTOR-ORIENTED COMMUNICATION

Another congruity between contemporary mission and the electronic media is that both engage in receptor-oriented communication. Contrary to the popular stereotype cross-cultural missionaries have to be sensitive to local cultures if they are to be effective. Bible translation, for example, requires persons to learn dynamic equivalents in another language. In doing so the focus shifts from the presenter to the receiver.[11]

Charles H. Kraft of the School of World Mission, Fuller Theological Seminary, is representative today of missiologists who appropriate the same communications theory which influences the television producers.[12] Kraft combines biblical studies, anthropological theory, and the insights of communications science in developing twelve models for relating Christianity and culture. From biblical theology he draws the images of God active in revelation in every culture in a dynamic, continuing communications process. In this view God desires to see Christian meanings communicated through human cultural forms including various languages. Each culture has its own validity, yet none is static. Worldview change is to be expected. Thus the missionary does not "corrupt" a traditional culture either by presence or message, for that culture inevitably is undergoing change.

Receptor-oriented communication is to be the goal. The Bible translator, for example, searches diligently for dynamic equivalents, symbols with "substantial correspondence between the intent of the communicator and the understanding of the receptor."[13] Kraft also writes of "communication with impact." That means that effective communications includes both cognitive and affective dimensions. If a message is intended simply to convey information, it does not have to relate closely to the felt needs of the hearer. But if the communicator hopes to influence a change in behavior, the communication must relate to felt needs if change is to result. This world-affirming, culture-affirming perspective is also media-affirming. With his goal of "high impact communication," Kraft is open to new communications technologies. Just as Bible societies adopted the latest technologies, from wooden to metal type, and from linotype to offset to laser printing, so other mission communicators not only receive new electronic media technologies, but affirm them as God-given.

Just as the communications specialist in world mission has grown sensitive to the pluralities of receiving groups, so also media specialists have developed sensitivities concerning their varied audiences. As the sociologist Eliot Freidson pointed out, the notion of "mass" as applied to mass communications is contrary to a great deal of empirical data. Communications researchers find repeatedly how important informal communications is in modern society. Studies after World War II showed that Allied propaganda directed at German troops was largely ineffective since individuals tended to reject that which would separate them from their in-group. A Nielsen study in 1985 disclosed that each television evangelist speaks to a discrete audience.[14] Those holding to a market-driven approach to the media would gratify audience wants and needs without reference to values. Others are in reaction against the implied values of avarice, lust, greed and violence presented in both television advertizing and programming. People like Michael Schudson, concerned primarily for the quality of human life and relationships, remain hopeful that advertising and television programming can be arts that enhance human and humane values.[15]

> **A theology of mission which affirms God's revelatory work in every culture can be at the same time receptor-oriented, culture- and technology-affirming.**

Does "receptor-oriented revelation" merely reinforce the incipient tribalism of each local community? Does it tend to thwart efforts for convergences and a wider sense of community? Or is it possible to think globally while acting locally? As a response to the UNESCO debate on a New World Information and Communication Order, the World Council of Churches published stories of nine communications ventures in which Christians both critiqued existing media structures and demonstrated that specific media technologies can be instruments of liberation, change and renewal. Martin Marty in his theological reflection suggests Christians ought to employ media for the sake of seeking convergences, for developing larger community out of sub-communities. He believes that we face a real choice, either to surrender to the limits of specialization, or to imitate those who are making efforts to transcend tribe.[16]

Thinking of the electronic media in this way, we are reminded of that technician of impressionist painting, Georges Seurat. He developed pointillism, a method of putting the pigment on the canvass in tiny round dots of about equal size with scientific precision as to the color relation of dot to dot. Did such precision of minute parts detract from the effectiveness of the whole? By no means. Concerning his masterpiece, *La Grande Jatte*, a critic wrote that light, air, people and landscape are frozen into an abstraction in which line, color, color values and shapes cohere into an organization as precisely as the parts of a machine. A calculating, intellectual art is this -- in no sense a mechanical procedure, but an art which moves by its serene monumentality.[17] The local and the global are complementary and not antithetical. A theology of mission which affirms God's revelatory work in every culture can be at the same time receptor-oriented, culture- and technology-affirming.

DISSONANCES AND DEMOCRATIC COMMUNICATION

Thus far we have noted basic congruity between missiology and the electronic media. Nevertheless, there are underlying dissonances between liberation theologies of mission which are praxis-oriented and many contemporary uses of electronic media. These include issues of media distribution, control and sensitivity to human needs, especially of the poor and dispossessed.

Should market forces determine television content and accessibility? What of basic human rights and fundamental social needs as values to consider? Dr. George Moser, President of the Communication Commission of the German Catholic Bishops' Conference, argues that communications media are not a product to be distributed according to political and commercial considerations. Instead he believes that the value of free expression of opinion requires that all, including social, ideological and ethnic minority groups, should be able to articulate their concerns.[18] He raises two ethical issues which affect both global media and Christian mission, viz., just distribution and just control.

The issue of just distribution of scarce communications resources exists in both affluent and poor countries. It concerns in the U.S. and other countries, for example, the allocation of cable television stations and satellite channels. These issues also affect churches in countries of the two-thirds world. Hugo Assmann, the noted Brazilian theologian, writes of the electronic church and its impact in Latin America. For Assmann communication is fundamentally between persons. However, since communication is conditioned by the historically determined situation of society, it cannot be isolated from the global social context. The fact is that the poor of Latin America have almost no access to programming on television in that continent.[19]

In 1985 UNESCO carried out a detailed study of media in Latin America. As expected they found that electronic media, specifically radio and television, had replaced print media as the most influential means of shaping opinions, attitudes, beliefs and values. Four trends were identified. First, there was heavy radio penetration in both rural and urban areas of all countries. Concerning the latter it was noted that by the year 2000, 82 percent of Latin America's population will be concentrated in cities. Second, they found a spectacular growth of television, measured both by the amount of investment in advertising and the leisure time devoted to viewing, with a corresponding stunted development of the press in the region. Third, they found an imbalance between private and public sectors in their control over radio and television, with the former dominating without appropriate regulation. Finally, they noted a low level of local program production and a strong dependence on program imports.[20]

The imbalance in distribution of media resources between the rich and poor nations parallels that of economies as a whole. During the 1960s nations of the two-thirds world called for a New International Economic Order. At the same time they brought to the United Nations their appeal for a New International Information Order. UNESCO has been the forum for ongoing discussions. In 1980 a study commission headed by Sean MacBride presented its report. Instead of victors and victims it disclosed a "technological dilemma." On the one hand the MacBride Commission recommended rapid development of communications technology in countries of the two-thirds world. On the other hand it warned of the profound impact of such new technologies on local cultures.[21]

Closely related to the issue of just media distribution is that of just control, who controls the media. World mission leaders join today in concern over the disproportionate control of information media by the governments and corporations of first world nations. Consider these facts from the MacBride Commission as summarized by Fr. Michael Traber, Secretary of the World Association for Christian Communication:

> The countries of the West have a near monopoly in the international dissemination of information: the world receives some eighty per cent of its news through London, Paris and New York....The main instrument of the North's domination of communication are the transnational communication corporations. The principal objective of transnational corporations is the maximization of profit....The intrusion of computer and micro-electronic technologies, linked through satellites, into the global information system is likely to make the world's imbalance in information almost irreversible.[22]

In response to this issue the World Council of Churches at its Sixth Assembly (Vancouver 1983) called for a more participatory media system. Delegates were deeply conscious of the uneven distribution of media growth and the control of those media by a few powerful countries and transnational corporations. The assembly called for the creation of decentralized, community-based, local media outlets.

Assmann documents the near-monopoly of U.S. televangelists in religious broadcasting in Latin America. They tend to have their own broadcast stations, interconnections and guaranteed access to satellite connections. They raise funds within Latin America in various ways, from selling advertising space, religious trinkets and "club" memberships, to threats to suspend programming due to low donations. Is there a danger of Yankee imperialism in television evangelism? Assmann gives an emphatic "yes"! A near autocracy exists in televangelism with power centralized in a few. But it is the marriage of religious autocracy with the ruling political elite that most concerns him. For him the electronic church in Latin America should be seen as a movement of idolatry, having a profound and organic relation with the secular oppressive systems in South and Central America.[23]

In another detailed study of televangelism in Latin America, Dennis Smith investigated the pastoral and ideological impact of evangelical broadcasting on Central American Christians. In a region torn by struggles of the oppressed for economic and political justice, he found that both U.S. televangelists and local radio evangelists did not question the political or economic status quo. Their religious impact, on the other hand, has been considerable. Large numbers of persons now identify themselves as evangelicals. Sincere persons testify to transformed personal lives and the influence of the religious media upon them. "But not all the fruits have been sweet," Smith concludes. "Bitter sectarianism, isolationism, individualism, crass materialism and alienation from the historical processes at work in society are also characteristic of Central American evangelicals."[24]

PERSON-CENTERED COMMUNICATION

Thus far we have analyzed both congruences and dissonances between global mission and electronic media. The fundamental question remains. Are these inconsistencies inherent in the technology of the electronic media? Are there options for use of the television media that have a potential for social transformation? If so they can play a positive role in the churches' mission when conceived broadly to include both personal and social salvation.

In communications theory today a search is taking place for a new paradigm of person-centered communication. Robert A. White, Research Director of the Centre for the Study of Communication and Culture in London, England, argues that that search is measured "in terms of its ability to enhance our respect for the dignity and freedom of the person and to enable persons to work peacefully and justly for the common welfare." White believes that such a paradigm "provides a conceptual base for worldwide movement toward the democratization of communication."[25]The way forward begins with the recognition that the medium of television is a combination of technology **and** social institutions. Technology always is used within a framework of social institutions composed both of actors and of social norms. To these premises theologians of the church's mission would add their conviction that God is actively at work in mission, seeking both the salvation of individuals and the redemption of social institutions. God who can make all things new can use both the technology of the media and the communicators in the work of redemption.

Roman Catholic communicators in Latin America and the Caribbean have called for media which are person-centered. In doing so they identified three issues for those concerned to develop communications with "the human dimension": First, to make out of communications, and even out of the new technologies, means of expression, dialogue and participative communication; second, to find in communications the possibility of feeling and perceiving reality objectively as the creative self-expression and, consequently, encounter and communion among human beings; and third, to make communications a transforming factor both of one's own self and of social reality. While admittedly utopian this statement is based on the theological assumptions discussed above, namely, that God is pro-active in all contemporary cultures in creation and redemption of the world, including the world of media.

The World Council of Churches at its Vancouver Assembly in 1983 also proposed a person-centered approach to media. Where new media systems are not established, it recommended an active search for those media which are indigenous and which the people can own and manage, for example, drama, oral literature, music, cassettes and film. These are what the Latin American Episcopal Conference at Puebla in 1979 called "group media" in contrast to "mass media." The Vancouver Assembly called on the churches to affirm the basic human right to communicate where participation by the people in the media is denied by oppressive political forces.

The Vancouver statement on "Communicating Credibly" contained the following questions concerning credibility. Together they are an appropriate summary of the questions which missiologists and specialists in Christian communications are raising: First, intention: what is the motivation of the communication? Does it affirm or exploit the people? Are cultural differences being respected. Second, content: does the communication make peace, build justice and promote wholeness? Does it present a complete picture, or is it based on national or sectarian prejudice? Third, style: does the communication have clarity, economy, precision, variety and a sense of humor? Fourth, dialogue: does the receiver have the opportunity to respond or is the communication totally one-way? Does communication listen, as well as speak? Does it call for informed choice and active response to the issues presented? Does it respect the reality of pluralism and provide for the voicing of diverse views? Fifth, appropriateness: is the form of the communication appropriate and does the choice of media suit the task? To these the authors "from a Christian perspective" add two more. Sixth, mystery: does the communication respect the "otherness" of the gospel by refusing to explain everything and by avoiding quick judgments? Seventh, value reversal: does the communication reflect the gospel's reversal of the normal order of importance and value; that is, the last before first, foolish before wise, weak before powerful, poor before rich?[26]

The practical question remains. Are there effective models of such a person-centered approach to media communication? Consider first the styles of communication in churches undergoing renewal. In his thesis on the new consciousness of the church in Latin America, Ronaldo Munoz of Chile declares that two models of the church exist side by side. The first is the model of the great institutional church. It's center is among the rich and power-

Creative options in electronic media do exist for churches to tell their story in person-centered, authentic ways.

ful, and not among the poor for whom it organizes charity. This church has power to negotiate with those in political and military authority, and tries to ameliorate the social conditions under which many suffer. It teaches doctrine with authority and can make itself heard through mass media of communication. The second model Munoz calls the communications-network church. It has its sociological and cultural center among the poor. In it fellowship is celebrated and responsibility shared. It seeks to bear witness to the gospel in humble ways with intense and frequent person-to-person contact and communication, in which deep feelings are shared and mutual ministries exercised. Among Roman Catholics such intentional communities for transformation are called "base Christian (or ecclesial) communities."[27]

Often today in the midst of varied forms of suffering, new communities of *shalom* are being born. They experience God as present with them as the suffering Christ and the living Holy Spirit. Out of injustice blossoms new faith and hope. Theirs is a "tough story" but one which in its telling unites suffering peoples of faith. Could such communities find alternative ways to use electronic media? Dennis Benson says "yes"! He calls his new approach "interactive videos."

In *The Visible Church* Benson describes three insights gained from visits to seven of the fastest growing churches in a major North American denomination. First, each church demonstrated that it was a caring church in the community. Members did not confine their witness to worship in the sanctuary, but took their faith to the streets. Second, the laity shared powerfully in the ministry of the church. Third, the clergy understood their enabling roles. The whole body of Christ provides the spark for renewal and outreach. Benson gives fourteen models by which viewers of media can become active participants, and in the process equip themselves for authentic mission and ministry.[28] Others would propose narrowcasting in which local parishes produce television programs about their own communities. Still others would provide study groups with discussion guides for simultaneous response to selected television programs. A bonding can take place among peoples, even across East and West and North and South divides, when the peoples' story is communicated effectively. One example was the Maryknoll film *Consuming Hunger* which competed with Nova and other television network productions and won the 1988 World Hunger Media Award bestowed by the World Hunger Year. Creative options in electronic media do exist for churches to tell their story in person-centered, authentic ways.

CONCLUSION

An Indonesian delegate to the World Council of Churches' Vancouver Assembly expressed well this concern that electronic media for authentic communication be people-centered as he wrote:

> In the depth of silence
> no words are needed,
> no language required.
> In the depth of silence
> I am called to listen.
> > Yes, there I sat
> > there in that corner,
> > listening for silence,
> > longing for community.
> Suddenly the room is crowded,
> crowded with speeches
> voices in many languages
> > announcing
> > denouncing
> > proclaiming
> > demanding
> > self-justifying

shattering the silence.
Christian communication must announce
No, Christian communication must denounce,
No, Christian communication must promote sharing,
No, Christian communication must create community,
Yes, Christian communication must be hopeful
No, it must be graceful
Yes, it must have integrity
No, it must call for response.
>Please stop, please!
>Silence!
>Listen to the beating of your heart
>Listen to the blowing of the wind,
>the movement of the Spirit,
Be silent -- said the Lord,
>and know that I am God.
And listen to the cry of the voiceless
Listen to the groaning of the hungry
Listen to the pain of the landless
Listen to the sigh of the oppressed
>and to the laughter of children.
For that is authentic communication:
>listening to people
>living with people
>dying for people.[29]

DONALD B. ROGERS

"Television changes the perceptual set of the people we are working with. They see differently. It's a matter of time, of intensity. You don't look at the world the same after you have been television-ized. People walk into the church, into the classroom, into any kind of relationship and bring that perceptual set with them. If this isn't taken into account, if we treat people as if they are in some more traditional interpretative pattern, then we are simply out of touch and don't reach them."

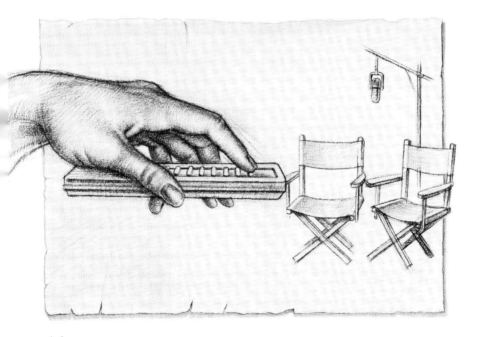

“ *If I could produce any television program I wanted, the core of it would be interviews with unknown, interesting people. I'd give them their Andy Warhol 'fifteen minutes of fame.' I find it fascinating when people do street interviews, not just quips, but sit down with somebody and talk to them.* **”**

145

"With television attention span moves quickly. Intimacy is instant, necessitating education now to be very intimate. You can't do big stuff unless you have somehow bridged the gap. For instance, watch Jimmy Swaggart. While one gets a sense that he is speaking to ten thousand people, the camera makes it seem that you and Jimmy are doing this. It raises the intimacy level; it lowers the attention span. The music is hot, the color is hot, issuing an intensity that makes it difficult to relax out of it. One has a hard time letting something go slow. Silence is threatening. Slow-paced stuff is threatening because it is strange. Also, I would never underestimate the voyeur interest of the human being. Television and radio are voyeur media."

"I don't feel guilty at all when I watch television. I watch it as a escape as much as anything. So I watch all the channels at once. As a result I have to watch it alone, because no one else can stand the channel flipping. There is something about its entirety that is sort of mind boggling. It is all on at once, from local cable broadcast religion, which is really interesting, to slick religious camera, and all the other stuff. They are selling stuff, constant news, weather. The whole is really more than the sum of its parts when you graze. I can't imagine anybody watching just one program."

"I don't want to talk to the rich and famous. I don't want to talk to the historically famous. I want to talk to the interesting, the bizarre, the characters of ordinary life. I'd provide interludes of film where you are in a low-flying airplane flying across the earth. You'd see a fantastic view of nature and reality without comment: we'd just look at it as it comes. Take off from some place and turn on the camera and see what is there. The plane roars across the landscape and you see fantastic beauty, traditional beauty, as well as the beauty of stuff that is ugly."

CHAPTER EIGHT

MAINTAINING FAITH IDENTITY IN A TELEVISION CULTURE: STRATEGIES OF RESPONSE FOR A PEOPLE IN EXILE

Donald B. Rogers

> The quantum vacuum, then, is a seething ocean, out of which virtual particles are constantly emerging and into which they constantly subside. And this is not merely an abstraction but a practical reality; as the American physicist Charles Misner notes: "There is a billion dollar industry -- the TV industry -- which does nothing except produce in empty space potentialities for electrons, were they to be inserted there, to perform some motion. A vacuum so rich in marketable potentialities cannot properly be called a void; it is really an ether."[1]

A MILDLY HOSTILE ENVIRONMENT

Today the people of faith find themselves once again the minority in a mildly hostile cultural environment. The environment is hostile in that it presents patterns, values and symbols that are in significant dissonance with those envisioned and put forth by the faith community. It is mild, and infuriatingly so, in that the culture finds little in the way of faith that must be feared, little that needs to be admired, much that can be ignored. The cultural environment and its institutional as well as private expressions and embodiments are complete on their own terms, including the means by which the cultural values are translated into symbol systems and transmitted, fraught with valenced powers, to others. Those others who receive and are wooed and pressured into conformity are those of both the next generation and the present generations. The media are agencies of that transmission. Broadcast television is part of that media complex.

Broadcast television, commercially based for the main part, is neither the devil nor the savior of the minority culture of faith. It is, rather, a highly significant means of cultural perpetuation and transformation, essentially empty in and of itself, a means that is significant in its usage far more than in its own character. Like the automobile the very fact of its existence creates possibilities and problems. The parish church life-patterns, for example, have been significantly, and in some ways negatively, modified by the existence of the automobile. People no longer have to worship where they live. The parish church is no longer tied to its neighborhood and can ignore that neighborhood's problems.

In a similar way television affects the way of life of the faith by its possibilities. But the more relevant first analysis is the exploration of the ways in which a medium of mass communications becomes the vehicle of cultural life. The second analysis is of the strategies available to the people of faith in response to a mildly hostile culture and the means that culture uses to nurture its own life. How did, how can the people of faith live in exile?

LIVING IN EXILE

Our thesis is that the people of faith can understand their current situation and examine their options more clearly by sensing that, without having traveled, they are now living as did the people of the Exile. The dynamics of that time can help us to understand our relationship to the current cultural situation, help us to develop strategies for life in the our times, and bring both Exodus and Exile into our Easter.

Exile is not Exodus. Exile and Exodus are not Easter. All of these are dominant metaphors of the life of the people of faith in the biblical tradition. The latter two are used often in the imaging of the life of the people of faith today. The Exile is relatively neglected. Its neglect may be, in part, because that long experience and its impact on the content of much of the Old Testament, is unattractive to a culture that is more than a little influenced by heroic impulses. Exile differs from Exodus in that the driving force of Exodus is the hope for and experience of a flight to freedom from a hostile land. Exodus requires that there be a promised land to go to, one that may have to be wrested away from its present occupants, but one which is so clearly mandated as the possession of the people of faith that such aggression is legitimized.

Such an option no longer exists. There is no believably open promised land to which we can flee. Nor is there any homeland that we can hope to return to either by invasion in force or reclamation by infiltration. We live in exile and we shall in the future. The prospects are humbling. The triumphalism that has taken over Easter and been pushed to prominence in Exodus is, at best, a future reality that requires a divine intervention of revelatory dimensions. Only in an eschatologically proposed New Land, New Jerusalem or New World that God may create can such an Exodus resolution of cultural tensions be envisioned. That is the only place where the triumphalistic strategy of cultural victory is appropriate. In the meantime we live in Exile, and the culture around us is and will be the condition of our future.

It is not necessary to recite at length the dissonance between the cultural values and life patterns of the people of faith and the values and life patterns of the current dominant culture. If that assumption about our situation is not accurate, if dissonance is seen to be non-existent or of no particular significance for faith, then the relationship of the people of faith to the media promoting that culture is equally insignificant. If we live in harmony to a sufficient enough degree that we need not be concerned, then the strategy that recommends itself is one of simple linear continuation. Only if there is some significant variance between our ideals and that which we see promoted by cultural forces through the media of television do we need to be concerned.

TELEVISION AS THE VERNACULAR

There is one exception. Even in a harmonious world where the way of faith and the way of the cultural setting are highly compatible, the church may find it necessary or advisable to recognize that the vernacular is defined outside of the community of faith. The language of any people is seldom contained by the dictionaries of their religion since the tendency of religious language is toward unique definitions that explain its own mysteries. Religionists translate the special and private language into the vernacular. Thus for any religion where there is a desire to participate in culture in open communication, even without a desire to save people from its clutches or transform the entirety, the necessity of translation requires a knowledge of the vernacular language defined by others. Television is one, if not the major, cultural dictionary of our time. It is a particularly powerful dictionary in that it is active, multi-sensory, imaginative, ubiquitous, intimate and repetitious.

Television is only a secondary force in the creation of language. By its very commercial nature, dependent upon an audience acceptance, the final determination of the content of the definitions of the dictionary has a much broader cultural base. Television tests, experiments and transmits the constantly revising language. Its power is not in an isolated creativity, but in the effectiveness of its transmissions. That is why we list its power as being a matter of the combined impact of active, multi-sensory, imaginative, ubiquitous, intimate and repetitious nature.

Television is **active** and intrudes into life. To be sure people must turn the set on, but once on, it is no longer a passive presence. It calls for attention, pleads and demands that attention through technical and programmatic devices. Television has an activity dimension unlike the printed page, and beyond that of radio or film.

Television is **multi-sensory**, using more of the sensory avenues than most other media. It is simply a rich combination of color and movement and sound, ready to practice the delightful freedom of artistic deception. Just as all art has communicated truth as well as falsehood through the use of conventions of deception, so television portrays realities through unrealities, and vice versa, in a media language that is understood in many sensory dimensions. It is not the technical language that we need to know. It is not the language only of the technique of television production that we must understand. It is the cultural language, the new definitions in image and conno- tation and nuance as well as specific dictionary-like delineation, that is communicated by a technical language that is powerfully multi- sensory and holistic.

Television is powerful through its dependence upon the **imagi- nation** of the viewer.[2] As an art form television depends upon the viewers to create inside of their own minds the supplementary realties that are not shown on the face of the tube. Some are concerned that television has a negative effect at precisely this point. They say that television damp- ens the imaginative abili- ties by being so explicit in its portrayals. Those who used to "watch" radio programs, able to see what the sounds suggested, and those who delight in imaginative interaction with printed texts sense that television is less rich in this respect. That may be so. But while television may differ in the way in which it makes appeals to the imagination, as does film or liturgical activity, it none the less gets its power in part from the appeal made to the imagination of the viewer, imagination responding to what is sometimes almost pure image.

> **Exile called for a strategy of quixotic character, rather than heroic, a strategy of comedic tendencies rather than tragic.**

The cultural power of television is directly related to its nearly **universal** presence. The studies indicate that television sets are more prevalent than indoor plumbing, automobiles and any other modern appliance. Television sets are in use across all the statistical divisions of society. It is now a matter of snobbery to maintain that one does **not** own a set, or never turns it on except to watch an edu- cational program. This ubiquity means the communication of a cultural language is nearly instantaneously universal. The language is known not only "across America," but across all the Americas and all other continents as well. One expects to see satellite dishes in the background of *National Geographic* pictures of remote tribal loca- tions. Around the clock, present nearly everywhere instantane- ously, television is ubiquitous.

Ironically this dictionary of a world-wide cultural language is **intimate,** more appropriately experienced alone or in small groups. In this sense television is not a public media as much as it is a broadly dispersed private media. It is appropriately small, room sized, near and as loud or as soft as, usually, one person desires. Television will sit by one's bedside in the nursing home or hospital, be the sole "other" occupant of one's living room, accompany one's meals, go with one to the cabin or beach. It has all the seductive power of the private conversation or the confessional. Others have noted that, in this intimacy, television has made public that which formerly was regarded as private, and made private that which was formerly made public. This reversal is in itself a re-writing of the language.

Its power is also a matter of **repetition.** This dimension of television has not been adequately explored. It seems apparent that repetition is one of the key elements to understanding the power television has in shaping a culture through the distribution to and education of great portions of the populace in the language of a culture. The commercial advertisers display this commitment to repetition quite well. For good reason they want their commercials to be repeated many times in order to communicate their message. That it works is evidenced by the memorization of commercials that takes place among people who unconsciously, sometimes to their own dismay, learn the lyrics and actors and logos of the products. Similarly significant is the learning of the details of complete series that occurs through the re-run phenomenon. The motivation of the broadcasting industry at this point is probably to make more money without having to incur production costs. The effect is that patterns of life, "Star Trek" to "Mr. Ed," "Upstairs/Downstairs" to "The Honeymooners" are digested in detail. Knowing that "once is not enough" television is powerfully repetitious.

As a cultural language dictionary television operates with effective technique. This is its **how.** When its **content** becomes the object of our exploration, we are immediately confronted with the much larger hermeneutical problem. The cultural language that television inculcates is knowable only in its details, and only for today. That is an over-statement, but the point is that learning the language of one's own time has become a challenging task because of the specificity of the definitions and the transitory character of the symbols. Jack Solomon chose to illustrate his chapter on the role television plays in defining the cultural symbols of our time by referring to five shows, only one of which was still on the air when his book got into print.[3] The shows that replaced the cancelled shows may not be much different except in packaging, and one might argue that the way television stays the same is by constantly changing. Innovation is one way to preserve attention to what is in essence the same old stuff.

Solomon illustrates that a major thrust of television drama productions, in the sit-coms and the serious dramatic series, is the definition of gender roles.[4] It is equally evident that those same productions define what it means to be a certain age (child, youth, young adult, elderly), what its means to be urban,rural or suburban. Other less tangible definitions refer to successful, attractive, good, competent, and on and on. The dimensions of humanness and human life that are defined are, not incidentally, dimensions of the life of faith as well.

Solomon's book is significant to this discussion in that he shows that the impact of television on the cultural language systems of our time is in part due to its reflective quality, or echoing effect. That is, television of the broadcast variety in particular is market driven and sensitive to the acceptance level of its viewers. Often, then, what television does is confirm a linguistic change of direction rather than consciously seek to change that language. Television is powerful in so far as it is compatible with a symbol creating/defining pattern that includes forces such as advertising of all sorts, architecture, toys, clothing, food, magazines and radio. Television is most accurately understood as a purveyor of the operative vernacular language systems when it is seen as but one part of the complex of cultural language formation.

> **We are teaching students how to compose when our students do not yet know the standard repertoire.**

Therein lies the difficulty we have in stating what the church does or should think of television. Television is not an isolated cultural force. It is only one part of a complex system, even though a highly significant part, most notable as an echoing device for meanings that find their rootage elsewhere in cultural dynamisms. Television cannot be isolated from that larger cultural mixture. Our thesis so far is that even in a time and place when there might be great compatibility between the language of faith and the language of culture, it would still be necessary to learn to read the ever changing vernacular in all of its expressions, including in our day the television forms. We do this in order to carry out what some see as a desirable dialogue with the people of one's cultural milieu, and what others see as a theologically necessary conversation.

For some people of the community the communication of the faith to all in the language of the people is a necessary activity. They maintain we **must** learn that language, and television is one of our dictionaries. If, on the other hand, we maintain that we are living in an exilic condition, where the predominant cultural language will reflect dissonant and perhaps antagonistic points of view, interpretations, meanings, values and patterns of living, then we are required to expand our strategy of relating to television. How shall we live in a foreign land and how shall we sing the Lord's songs?

THE CHURCH'S RESPONSE TO EXILE

Our reading of the complex pattern of response to the Exile in the Old Testament records is this. The Exile became, not without some internal struggles, a time for walking a tight-rope in a foreign culture without the loss of one's cultural/faith identity. The Exile became a time of humble yet determined waiting for a future that would become the reality only for subsequent generations. It was a time that avoided, for the most part, a hostile relationship to the surrounding culture, subversionary strategies, conversionary ambitions, isolationist entombments and flight. Exile called for a strategy of quixotic character, rather than heroic, a strategy of comedic tendencies, rather than tragic. The people of faith were advised by their eventually accepted prophets to make the best of their plight and live productively in great interaction with their captors. They were urged to maintain tenaciously the ritual and educational activities that communicated the richest parts of their past to the next generations, to construct new institutions to perform those tasks if necessary and someday, when God should choose to act, to return, reinhabit and rebuild.[5]

What does this view suggest for developing strategies for our day as the people of faith find their way in the midst of a mildly hostile culture, displayed and inculcated in part by the media of broadcast television?

First, we do not and will not control the definitions of the cultural languages. The vernacular is not ours to define. We must know that language well, engage it critically as opportunities arise or are created, but do so with no great expectation that our work will ever be done. The language that television uses will never be ours.

Second, some of our most useful and precious terms will be lost beyond redemption. In order to distinguish our meanings from the cultural meanings, we may have to change our private language rather than expect the cultural participants to revise their language to accommodate our tradition. That is, we will respond to television by a conscious re-development of a private language to be taught to the initiated, while struggling to do an as accurate as possible translation of the faith language into the vernacular. Instead, for example, of waging a battle that says we and we alone have the true definition of "love," and that others should recognize our superiority of understanding and be more precise when they use that term, we may have to retreat more and more to an "agape" terminology in order to attain the goal of differentiation.

Third, we will see that television is only one part of a larger complex, not especially by nature contrary to our own ideals and activities, fully open in principle to our own usage, but matter-offactly the property of others. We may choose to compete in the broadcast television arena from time to time for symbolic reasons, but we will be wasting our time trying to correct the content of its programming.

Fourth, we will teach our children cultural-criticism skills, including the skills for "reading the tube" as both a defensive/protective strategy and as a commission for fulfilling a translation strategy. We will teach them, and ourselves in the process, so that we, wise in the ways of the world, can be free from unknowing capitulation or useless isolation.

Fifth, we will teach the past of our faith with a renewed intentionality in order to equip our own community with the clarity of identity necessary to live in the midst of these days. Furthermore, we will not practice isolationism, subversion, rebellion or flight from our cultural time nor its means of communication. Neither will we allow our minds and hearts and souls to become captive to the cultural environment that surrounds us.

Finally, we will remember how to sing the Lord's songs in a foreign land. We will teach those songs to others. Living where we are we will turn on our television sets, read our world, and from time to time, see ourselves there on the electronic tube with full faithful integrity. We may never make it to MTV, desirable as that might be, but we can sing our songs and live our faith in this world.[6]

IMPLICATIONS FOR RELIGIOUS EDUCATION

The implications of this for religious education, at the parish level or the seminary level, are matters of content and skills. The shift in emphasis would be toward a more thorough grounding in the tradition combined with a sharpening of ethnographic-semiotic abilities. We are not far from the supposed advice of Karl Barth that we learn to read the Bible in one hand and the newspaper in the other.

The Exilic emphasis that gave birth to the synagogue instructional system was upon the deepening of the preparation of the next generation in the solid core materials of the Judaic tradition. It became very important for that tradition to be carried into the future by some who knew it very well. Even the written records could no longer be trusted; another enemy might destroy them or force the community to place the sacred texts in hiding. The contents must be known by heart, and all the implications must be rehearsed with the wisdom of the wisest of the wise at hand.

This internalization of the tradition requires far more attention be given to the mastery of content than is currently the pattern at any level of Christian religious education. The suspicion that we have many illiterate believers, illiterate of the faith culture, is well grounded. Nothing seems to display the shallowness of the knowledge of the faith more than an increase in the technical abilities in broadcast media. The "nakedness" of thought that comes along with the cryptic nature of televised religion especially pushes into full view the nature of one's understanding of the faith as it leaves no room for the qualifying footnotes of talk in search of substance.

Television is impressionistic in the holistic form mentioned above, and the "message" is blatantly stated in the fullness of the details of that impression. The details, quickly presented, are consistent and, accurate or not, there is no time to go back for a second reading or ask for clarification.

Maintaining faith identity comes from an across the board thoroughness of basic knowledge in the substantive areas of religious education curriculum. Whereas we now move quickly to teach students how to do disciplinary tasks (how to do biblical exegesis or theology, for example), we may have to retreat into a pattern that takes first steps before second steps. We are teaching students how to compose when our students do not yet know the standard repertoire.

One skill area that we need to pay attention to is one that is not yet clearly formulated: the ability to read one's cultural setting accurately and specifically, with special attention to its meaning-carrying and value-carrying symbol systems. Practical theologians have dabbled in this area, maintaining that a promising contribution of their method will be in this direction. With the help that may be coming from the relatively new arena of semiotics, of which Jack Solomon is a representative, the ethnographic skills associated mostly with cultural anthropological investigation can be shaped to improve the skills of the laity and clergy alike in the understanding of our times. Interestingly enough semiotics places considerable emphasis upon the ordinary languages of our times, the cultural vernacular.[7]

With a faith identity more firmly rooted in an understanding of the best of the faith traditions and with the ability to see more clearly the variances and hear more sharply the dissonances between that identity and our cultural environment, which includes the institutions of the church, we will have prepared the people of faith and their mentors to live into an unknown cultural future.

AFTERWORD

Gregor Goethals

In contrast to high art, popular images today perform a legitimating function in American society, fulfilling a more indirect role that religion once played. Even today in compact societies where religious communities still confer or reinforce a sense of identity, religion performs a confirming, integrative role. In addition to its manifest, saving dimension, traditional religion has always offered an account of reality which enabled individuals and groups to place themselves in a social, as well as an eternal scheme of things. In advanced, pluralistic societies, however, this latent role of religion has been taken over by other authorities--political, economic, and scientific--which provide their constituencies with information, values, and identities.

In the United States the mass media have become extraordinarily powerful in their capacity to legitimate certain basic American values and convictions.[1] While most of us are thinking in the categories furnished by *TV Guide*, there is a deep level of symbolization which **all** programs collectively form. What we see and hear, without reflection, appear to be images of our world. Actually they make up a huge canopy of fabricated audio-visual signs which serve as common references for millions of Americans. Thus television images, particularly in the United States, are public, shared symbols that for many Americans answer the questions "Who am I?" and "Who are we?" Under this giant canopy of images all denominations and religious traditions are exposed to the same framing of reality.

A similar frame of reality was achieved in ancient and medieval art. While we may enshrine fragments of such sculpted forms and celebrate them today as "high art," they were, nevertheless, the popular, legitimating, integrative images at the time they were created. They communicated to ordinary, unlettered people their history and values. Climbing to the Acropolis, an Athenian citizen could stand at the base of the Parthenon and, looking up, see the images that identified common loyalties. Depicted on the frieze, for example, was the ceremonial event which honored the patron goddess Athena. Represented in relief sculpture were Athenian citizens who formed a procession and made their way through the city and up the sacred way to the temple and the statue of the goddess.

Today our friezes, the visual narratives of grandeur and perfection, may be found in popular art. Our mythological dramas, heros and heroines, and ideological visions are produced through the contemporary forms of soap operas, sit-coms, commercials, news and sports. Like the sculpted images on ancient and medieval architecture, the figures created by electronic impulses also portray values and ideologies; similarly, they may be as distanced from everyday life as were the earlier idealized pictures of ordinary men and women. Although separated by centuries of symbolic and technological revolutions, the beautiful people depicted on the Parthenon frieze and those represented in television commercials are comparably value laden. In both instances the visual images assist in performing the latent, legitimating role of religion: the framing of "reality," the shaping of a commonly understood world.

The symbols of an American public religion, fostered especially through television, radiate throughout the culture. Through this medium and other popular arts the nation is blanketed with mythic, informational and political images. Do seminaries and churches today emphasize the distinctiveness of their own symbols or have they become fused with the pervasive myths and civic rituals perpetuated through television?

Responses will undoubtedly vary, depending upon individual and group concerns, age and educational levels, political, economic, and ethnic factors, as well as liturgical practices. Religious institutions that are concerned with symbols and communications technology in American culture can best initiate changes if they understand ourselves, our values, and the events that impinge upon our lives. Without the ideological saturation of television it is hard to imagine how we would elect politicians, maintain the vast socio-economic system in which millions of individuals are enmeshed, or make choices about the environment. Though some intellectuals and religious groups may be disdainful of the medium, it has become a major force in the fabrication of public meaning and in the design of images to foster confidence and faith in institutional policies.

Do denominations have any radically different stories to tell? Since a vast, complex communications system encompassing radio, print, computers and television is necessary to maintain our way of life and foster faith in it as well, it is not at all clear that religious groups in America really want to tell any stories that run counter to a public faith. Are American churches and synagogues so comfortably situated underneath the canopy of the American Way that their traditional myths seem irrelevant, insignificant, or unimportant?

Certainly the messages of conservative denominations blend rather unobtrusively with the prevailing political ideology that has dominated American society over the past decade. On the other hand, if there are faith claims and loyalties that do not fit well under this canopy, how are alternative stories told? And where? To whom? In a country where religious freedom prevails, denominations are free to produce and circulate their own myths and principles of faith. With the rapid growth of VCR technology and cable companies perhaps different kinds of myths, symbols, and channels of communication will be available to concerned individuals and denominations. While the collective audience may be small in number, churches are free to produce and distribute audio-visual materials appropriate for their beliefs and values.

The reverse side of the media's capacity to frame shared beliefs and embody symbols of a public faith is its power to de-mystify, to undo meaning, and shake up commonly held assumptions. Alongside the iconifying power of the media is its capacity to become iconoclastic. In religious terms this suggests that, in addition to its priestly role of confirming belief, communications technology today can be used in a prophetic way. Historically the role of the prophets in Israel was to call the nation back to its basic principles. They boldly and fiercely drew attention to the defections of a nation under God and the social ills which had overtaken society. Similarly there has been a prophetic strain continuing in Christianity which attempted to judge social institutions and to critique culture in light of ethical concerns. Are there those in the media or elsewhere willing to assume the responsibility of prophet?

In focusing upon the latent religious function performed by mass media today, I have emphasized the power of contemporary communications technologies, underwritten by institutional sponsors, to construct images of authority. The purpose has been to draw attention to the symbolic worlds we enter when we go beyond the boundaries of everyday routines and try to think about our corporate life. Prior to the information revolution, public symbols that bridged personal and communal experience were located in city squares and cathedrals. Today, access to our abstract, larger "world" is found in mass media, as we read the newspaper, switch on the radio, turn on the television. Like medieval peasants who left their fields to gape at pictures in stone and glass authorized by ecclesiastics, we are equally dependent upon institutional images to explain the larger system to which we belong. Concerned theological educators and churches may try momentarily to step outside of the symbolic atmosphere that surrounds us, asking first, if there are alternative mythologies. At the same time, they may also keep a prophetic watch over the making of meaning and the forms that purport to explain how things are.

The chapters in this book initiate a rich, provocative discussion of mass media and encourage us to develop ways in which the arts can be integrated into the church and in which seminary students understand better the authoritative symbolic environment in which they expect to preach and teach. Through an examination of popular forms students may discover an encompassing ideological framework within which different religious groups co-exist. At the same time, seminaries may use their resources to create alternative symbols of faith and to offer a critique of cultural values and ideologies.

Rhode Island School of Design
Providence, Rhode Island

ENDNOTES

CHAPTER ONE

(pages 23-40)

THE PLACE OF TELEVISION
IN THE CHURCH'S COMMUNICATION

1 Marshall McLuhan, *Understanding Media: The Extensions of Man* (New York: Signet, 1964).
2 The mythology surrounding the communications revolution is discussed most lucidly and cogently in James W. Carey and John J. Quirk, "The Mythos of the Electronic Revolution," in James W. Carey, *Communication As Culture: Essays on Media and Society* (Boston: Unwin Hyman, 1989), pp. 113-141.
3 See Daniel Czitrom, *Media and the American Mind: From Morse to McLuhan* (Chapel Hill: University of North Carolina Press, 1982).
4 Quentin Schultze, "The Mythos of the Electronic Church," *Critical Studies in Mass Communication*, 4 (1987), pp. 245-261.
5 Ben Armstrong, *The Electric Church* (Nashville: Thomas Nelson, 1979), pp. 172-73.
6 Ibid., pp. 8-11.
7 Carey, "A Cultural Approach to Communication," in his *Communication As Culture*, pp. 13-36.
8 Harold Adams Innis, *The Basis of Communication* (Toronto: University of Toronto Press, 1951).
9 Harold Adams Innis, *Empire and Communication* (Oxford: Oxford University Press, 1950).
10 Nathan O. Hatch, *The Democratization of American Christianity* (New Haven: Yale University Press, 1989).
11 Neil Postman, *Amusing Ourselves to Death: Public Discourse in the Age of Show Business* (New York: Viking, 1985).
12 Kathleen Hall Jamieson, *Eloquence in an Electronic Age: The Transformation of Political Speechmaking* (New York: Oxford University Press, 1988).
13 Bruce Barron, *The Health and Wealth Gospel* (Downers Grove, IL: Inter-Varsity Press, 1987); Jill Dubish and Raymond Michalowski, "Blessed Are the Rich: The New Gospel of Wealth in Contemporary Evangelism," in Marshall W. Fiswick and Ray B. Browne, eds.,*The God Pumpers: Religion in the Electronic Age* (Bowling Green, OH: Bowling Green State University Popular Press, 1987), pp. 13-45; D. R. McConnell, *A Different Gospel* (Peabody, MA: Hendrickson Publishers, 1988).
14 Willow Creek Community Church is discussed in Barbara Dolan, "Full House at Willow Creek," *Time*, 6 March 1989, p. 60. Probably the best analysis of Schuller's ministry is Dennis Voskuil, *Mountains into Goldmines* (Grand Rapids: Eerdmans Publishing, 1983).
15 Here we must acknowledge Martin Buber's work, which has greatly influenced our thinking on these matters.

16 We have taken up these issues in "The Mythos of the Electronic Church."
17 Margaret Mead, *Culture and Commitment: A Study of the Generation Gap* (Garden City, NY: Natural History Press/Doubleday Company, 1970).
18 Czitrom, *Media and the American Mind.* Also see Dave Berkman, "Long Before Falwell: Early Radio and Religion -- As Reported by the Nation's Periodical Press," *Journal of Popular Culture,* 21 (Spring, 1988), pp. 1-11.
19 These issues are discussed in Stewart M. Hoover, *Mass Media Religion: The Social Sources of the Electronic Church* (Newbury Park, CA: Sage, 1988).

CHAPTER TWO

(pages 43-58)

CRUNCHING THE TRADITION: CHRISTIANITY AND TELEVISION IN HISTORICAL PERSPECTIVE

1 The term "crunching" is here an adaptation of computer jargon and is meant to denote "a useful mutilation of a message as it is subjected to and transmitted by a technical medium."
2 The formation of these types was influenced but not controlled by Max Weber's ideal authority types: traditional, rational-legal and charismatic. See Max Weber, *The Protestant Ethic and the Spirit of Capitalism* (New York: Scribners, 1958).
3 Selection has been made on the basis of presumable acquaintance of the general reader with these personalities. That they are all male is reflective of the widespread ignorance of the wide variety and great number of women who have occupied prophetic or "charismatic" roles of every type listed. This condition needs to be rectified but this is hardly the place to attempt it.

CHAPTER THREE

(pages 61-76)

A NEW PARADIGM FOR INTERPRETING THE BIBLE ON TELEVISION

1 For an excellent survey of the history of biblical interpretation, see Robert Grant and David Tracy, *A Short History of the Interpretation of the Bible,* 2d. ed. (Philadelphia: Fortress, 1985).
2 The relationship between changes in communications technology and the history of biblical interpretation has been discussed explicitly in two major historical investigations. See Elizabeth Eisenstein, *The Printing Press as an Agent of Change* (Cambridge: Cambridge University Press, 1979) and Brian Stock, *The Implications of Literacy* (Princeton: Princeton University Press, 1983).
3 Hans Frei's identification of the hermeneutical paradigm of "meaning as reference" which formed the basis for historical criticism is directly related to the

development of silent reading and the study of the Bible as a document in silence. *The Eclipse of Biblical Narrative* (New Haven: Yale University Press, 1974).

4 The most comprehensive studies of the church's adaptation to changes in communications technology are the works of Fr. Walter Ong. See, for example, his *The Presence of the Word* (New Haven: Yale University Press, 1967), and *Interfaces of the Word* (Ithaca: Cornell University Press, 1977).

5 The investigations of the relationship between oral and written culture are extensive. For an excellent bibliography on this area and a synthetic treatment of this literature in the context of this transition in early Christianity, see Werner Kelber, *The Oral and the Written Gospel* (Philadelphia: Fortress Press, 1983). For the role of oral and written scripture in the history of religion, see Harold Coward, *Sacred Word and Sacred Text:Scripture in World Religions* (Maryknoll: Orbis Press, 1988); William Graham, *Beyond the Written Word: Oral Aspects of Scripture in the History of Religion* (Cambridge: Cambridge University Press, 1987); and Miriam Levering, *Rethinking Scripture* (Albany: State University of New York Press, 1989).

6 See, for example, Eric Werner, *The Sacred Bridge* (New York: Columbia University Press, 1959), pp. 1-127, 329-372.

7 Lord and Perry's classic study of the oral poetry tradition of Yugoslavia made clear the intimate relationship between the recital of tales and music. See Albert Lord, *The Singer of Tales* (New York: Atheneum, 1965). For an excellent survey of recent research on oral poetry, see Ruth Finnegan, *Oral Poetry* (Cambridge: Cambridge University Press, 1977).

8 Eric Havelock, *Preface to Plato* (Cambridge: Harvard University Press, 1963).

9 Tyron Inbody, "Television as a Medium for Theology," in this book, pp. 82-83.

10 Ibid., p.83.

CHAPTER FOUR

(pages 79-94)

TELEVISION AS A MEDIUM FOR THEOLOGY

1 Walter Ong, *The Presence of the Word: Some Prolegomena for Cultural and Religious History* (Minneapolis: University of Minnesota Press, 1967), pp. 17-110.

2 Thomas Boomershine, "Religious Education and Media Change: A Historical Sketch," *Religious Education*, 82, 2 (Spring, 1987), pp. 269-278.

3 For a discussion of world building or world construction, see Peter Berger and Thomas Luckmann, *The Social Construction of Reality* (New York: Anchor Books, 1967), and Peter Berger, *The Sacred Canopy: Elements of a Sociological Theory of Religion* (New York: Anchor Books, 1969).

4 Marshall McLuhan, *Understanding Media: The Extensions of Man* (New York: Signet, 1964), p. 88. "Only alphabet cultures have ever mastered connected lineal sequences as pervasive forms of psychic and social organization."

5 Ibid., p. 108.

6 Robert Jenson, "The Church and Mass Electronic Media: The Hermeneutic Problem," *Religious Education,* 82, 2 (Spring, 1987), p. 284. See, also, George Lindbeck, *The Nature of Doctrine: Religion and Theology in a Postliberal Age* (Philadelphia: Westminster Press, 1984), p. 69.

7 Schubert Ogden, "What is Theology?" *On Theology* (New York: Harper and Row, 1986), Propositions 1-3. See, also, his *The Point of Christology* (New York:

Harper and Row, 1982), pp. 88-96.

8　Schubert Ogden, *Faith and Freedom: Toward a Theology of Liberation* (Nashville: Abingdon Press, 1979), chapter 1. See, also, James Cone's review of *Faith and Freedom* in *Perkins Journal*, XXXIII, 1 (Fall, 1979), pp.51-55.

9　Schubert Ogden, "The Nature and State of Theological Scholarship and Research," *Theological Education*, XXIV, 1 (Autumn, 1987), p. 120.

10　John Cobb, "Is Theology an Academic Discipline?" Lecture at United Theological Seminary, Dayton, Ohio, January 29, 1988. See, also, John Cobb and Joseph Hough, *Christian Identity and Theological Education* (Chico, CA: Scholars Press, 1985).

11　The relation of metaphorical theology as "a genre of theological reflection" both to the problem of meaning and truth and to dogmatic and philosophical theology is discussed by Sallie McFague, *Speaking in Parables: A Study of Metaphor and Theology* (Philadelphia: Fortress Press, 1974), pp. 2-4, 23-24, 38-39, 63-64, 80-88, 115, 139, 178-181. See, also, her *Metaphorical Theology: Models of God in Religious Language* (Philadelphia: Fortress Press, 1982), pp. ix-x, 22-26.

12　James Cone, *A Black Theology of Liberation* (Philadelphia: Lippincott, 1970), p. 17.

13　Rosemary Ruether, "What is the Task of Theology?" *Christianity and Crisis* (May 24, 1976), pp. 124-125.

14　McFague, *Speaking in Parables*, pp. 3, 177.

15　McFague, *Metaphorical Theology*, chapter 1.

16　See William Fore, *Television and Religion: The Shaping of Faith, Values, and Culture* (Minneapolis: Augsburg Press, 1987); Quentin Schultze, "The Mythos of the Electronic Church," *Critical Studies in Mass Communications*, 4 (1987), pp. 245-261; Barbara Hargrave, "Theology, Education and the Electronic Media," *Religious Education*, 82, 2 (Spring, 1987), pp. 219-230; Robert Jenson, "The Church and Mass Electronic Media."

17　Neil Postman, *Amusing Ourselves to Death* (New York: Penguin Books, 1985), chapter 4.

18　Neil Postman, "Critical Thinking in the Electronic Era," *The Kettering Review* (Winter, 1987), p. 47.

19　Ibid., p. 46.

20　Ibid., p. 41.

21　Ibid., p. 43.

22　Robert Bruinsma, "Television and Schooling: A Review of Neil Postman's Views, " *Christian Educators Journal* (October-November, 1988), p. 27. The same point is made by John Elias, "Religious Education in a Television Culture," *Religious Education*, 76, 2 (March-April, 1981), p. 197.

23　Ibid.

24　Dorothy Emmet, *The Nature of Metaphysical Thinking* (London: Macmillan, 1960), p. 194. See, also, Susan Langer, *Philosophy in a New Key: A Study in the Symbolism of Reason, Rite, and Art* (New York: Mentor Books, 1951).

25　Ong, *The Presence of the Word*, pp. 58-60.

26　McFague, *Speaking in Parables*, pp. 3, 23; and her *Metaphorical Theology*, pp. ix, 22-29.

27　Bernard Meland, *Faith and Culture* (London: George Allen Unwin, 1955), pp. 94-95.

28　Gregor Goethals, *The TV Ritual: Worship at the Video Altar* (Boston: Beacon Press, 1981), chapter 3.

29　Michael Goldberg, *Theology and Narrative: A Critical Introduction* (Nashville: Abingdon Press, 1982), p. 35.

CHAPTER FIVE

(pages 97-110)

APPROACHES TO TELEVISION
IN RELIGIOUS EDUCATION

1 Robert Allen, ed., *Channels of Discourse* (Chapel Hill: University of North Carolina Press, 1987), p. 1.

2 Taken from the Student's leaflet in "The Perfect Family?" session 7 of *Real and Unreal,* in the Senior High *Witness* curriculum, Augsburg, 1986, p. 2.

3 Selected from "Images of the Elderly," *Values and Visions Video Thematic Guide,* Cultural Information Services, 1986.

4 See Walter Ong, *The Presence of the Word: Some Prolegomena for Cultural and Religious History* (New Haven: Yale University Press, 1967), pp. 17-110. We do not mean to imply that Ong originated cultural designation on the basis of communication,but that we are operating from his distinctions. Indeed, in our century, Lewis Mumford may deserve a share of the credit for linking cultural organization to media type.

5 See Thomas Boomershine, "Religious Education and Media Changes: A Historical Sketch," in *Religious Education,* 82, 2 (Spring, 1987), p. 270.

6 Walter Ong, *Orality and Literacy: The Technologizing of the Word* (London: Methuen, 1982), p. 78.

7 Note Stanley Cavell's suggestion that viewing a film inherently invites us to share and discuss our understandings with compatriot viewers, while reading a book does not lead to this essential reaction. Cavell does not say no one should or does talk about books, only that the cinematic media experience somehow invites more communal engagement with the message. See his *The World Viewed* (Cambridge: Harvard University Press, 1979), pp. 9-11.

8 Allen, *Channels of Discourse*, p. 2.

9 Neil Postman, *Amusing Ourselves to Death* (New York: Penguin Books, 1985), pp. 78, 8.

10 H. Richard Niebuhr, *Christ and Culture* (New York: Harper and Row, 1951), p. 32. The Niebuhrian typology is used simply as a framework to differentiate and clarify the assumptions, motifs and methodologies of each religious education approach to television. Other ways of organizing the field may be equally valid, but this particular framework has been adopted since it is helpful in distinguishing approaches.

11 Marie Winn, *Unplugging the Plug-In Drug* (New York: Penguin, 1987), p. xiii.

12 Lewis, Mumford, *The Myth of the Machine* (New York: Harcourt, Brace, and World, 1966), p. 3.

13 Jacques Ellul argues that we accept televised images as constructions of reality which explain the world for us. See *The Humiliation of the World* (Grand Rapids: Eerdmans, 1985), pp. 139-147.

14 Winn, *Unplugging the Plug-in Drug*, pp. 6-16.

15 Tom Emswiler, *Making the Most of Video in Religious Settings* (Normal, IL: Wesley Foundation, 1985), p. viii-ix.

16 Ibid., pp. 1-4.

17 Marshall McLuhan, *Understanding Media: The Extensions of Man* (New York: Signet, 1964), p. 35.

18 Ronald Sarno, *Using Media in Religious Education* (Birmingham: Religious Education Press, 1987), pp. 17-19.

165

19 Ong, *The Presence of the Word*, pp. 287-324.
20 Sarno also considers film, the projected images one properly views in a large screen in a darkened theatre, but for the purpose of this paper, the focus will remain on his treatment of television alone.
21 McLuhan's "medium is the message" becomes "medium is the metaphor" for Postman, who maintains that the "forms of human conversation . . . have the strongest possible influence on what ideas we can conveniently express." Postman, *Amusing Ourselves to Death*, p. 6.
22 Ibid., p. 87.
23 Ibid., p. 114-115.
24 For Postman "media literacy" fails to raise crucial questions about "the cognitive biases and social effects" of media. Ibid., p. 154.
25 Ibid., pp. 160-163.
26 See Thomas Groome, *Christian Religious Education* (New York: Harper and Row, 1980).
27 See Paulo Freire, *Education for Critical Consciousness* (New York: Continuum, 1973).
28 Mary Elizabeth Moore, *Education for Continuity and Change* (Nashville: Abingdon, 1983).

CHAPTER SIX

(pages 113-127)

THE USE OF TELEVISION
BY INTERPRETIVE COMMUNITIES

1 Thomas Kuhn, The Structure of Scientific Revolutions, 2d ed., enlarged (Chicago: University of Chicago Press, 1970).
2 Erving Goffman, *Asylums: Essays on the Social Situation of Mental Patients and Other Inmates* (Garden City, NY: Doubleday Company, 1961).
3 Neil Postman, *Amusing Ourselves to Death* (New York: Penguin Books, 1985), p. 9.
4 Marshall McLuhan, *Understanding Media: The Extensions of Man* (New York: McGraw Hill, 1964).
5 Langdon Winner, *Autonomous Technology: Technics-out-of-Control as a Theme in Political Thought* (Cambridge: The MIT Press, 1977), pp. 313-14.
6 Ibid., p. 314.
7 Joshua Meyrowitz, *No Sense of Place: The Impact of Electronic Media on Social Behavior* (New York: Oxford University Press, 1985), p. 53.
8 Postman, *Amusing Ourselves to Death.*, p. 7.
9 Meyrowitz, *No Sense of Place*, p. 71.
10 Postman, *Amusing Ourselves to Death*, p. 43.
11 David Noble, *Forces of Production: A Social History of Industrial Production* (New York: Alfred Knopf, 1984), pp. 191-92.
12 Meyrowitz, *No Sense of Place*, p. 53.
13 Neil Smelser, *Social Change in the Industrial Revolution: An Application of Theory to the British Cotton Industry* (Chicago: University of Chicago Press, 1959).
14 Stanley Fish, *Is There a Text in This Class?* (Cambridge: Harvard University Press, 1980), pp. 307-8.

15 Ibid, p. 313.

16 Ibid., p. 314-15.

17 Ibid., pp. 315, 318.

18 Peter Berger and Thomas Luckmann, *The Social Construction of Reality* (Garden City, NY: Doubleday, 1967), p. 137.

19 Fish, *Is There a Text in This Class?* pp. 331, 332, 344.

20 George Barna and William McKay, *Vital Signs: Emerging Social Trends and the Future of American Christianity* (Westchester, IL: Crossway Books, 1984), p. 123.

21 John Dewey *The Public and Its Problems* (New York: Henry Holt, 1927), p. 98.

22 Ibid., p. 154.

23 Meyrowitz, *No Sense of Place*, p. 309.

24 Postman, *Amusing Ourselves to Death*, p. 87.

25 Stuart Ewen and Elizabeth Ewen, *Channels of Desire: Mass Images and the Shaping of American Consciousness* (New York: McGraw-Hill, 1982), pp. 262, 263.

26 John Thompson, *Studies in the Theory of Ideology* (Berkeley: University of California Press, 1984), p. 33.

27 Ibid., p. 30.

28 Lewis Mumford, *Technics and Civilization* (New York: Harcourt and Brace, 1934).

CHAPTER SEVEN

(pages 131-143)

TELEVISION AND THE CHURCH'S GLOBAL MISSION

1 David Hesselgrave, *Communicating Christ Cross-Culturally* (Grand Rapids: Zondervan, 1978), p. 406.

2 David Bosch, *Witness to the World: The Christian Mission in Theological Perspective* (Atlanta: John Knox Press, 1980), pp. 35-37.

3 "Methodological Issues in Liberation Theology," *Frontiers of Theology in Latin America*, edited by Rosino Gibellini (Maryknoll, NY: Orbis Books, 1979), pp. 43-44.

4 Juan Louis Segundo, *The Liberation of Theology* (Maryknoll, NY: Orbis Books, 1976), pp. 8-9.

5 Luis G. del Valle, "A Theological Outlook Starting from Concrete Events," *Frontiers of Theology in Latin America*, pp. 96, 98.

6 Jose Miguez Bonino, *Doing Theology in a Revolutionary Situation* (Philadelphia: Fortress Press, 1975), pp. 88-89.

7 *Doing Theology in a Divided World: Papers from the Sixth International Conference of the Ecumenical Association of Third World Theologians, January 5-13, 1983, Geneva, Switzerland*, edited by Virginia Fabella and Sergio Torres (Maryknoll, NY: Orbis Books, 1983), p. 189.

8 Marshall McLuhan, *Understanding Media: The Extensions of Man* (New York: New American Library, 1964), pp. 23-35, 20-21, and Marshall McLuhan and Bruce Powers, *The Global Village: Transformations in World Life and Media in the 21st Century* (New York: Oxford University Press, 1989), p. 92.

9 Hugo Assmann, *La Iglesia Electronica y su Impacto en America Latina* (San Jose, CR: Editorial Dei, 1987), pp. 121-23.

10 "Communication Versus Alienation: Latin American Challenge of WACC,"

Media Development, 31, 1 (1984), p. 18.

11 See Lamin Sanneh, *Translating the Message: The Missionary Impact on Culture* (Maryknoll, NY: Orbis Books, 1989).

12 Charles H. Kraft, *Christianity in Culture* (Maryknoll, NY: Orbis Books, 1979).

13 Ibid., p. 394.

14 Razelle Frankl, *Televangelism: The Marketing of Popular Religion* (Carbondale: Southern Illinois University Press, 1987), p. 146.

15 See Harry Skornia, *Television and Society: An Inquest and Agenda for Improvement* (New York: McGraw-Hill, 1965); Stuart Ewen, *The Captains of Consciousness: Advertizing and the Social Roots of the Consumer Culture* (New York: McGraw-Hill, 1976); and Michael Schudson, *Advertizing: The Uneasy Persuasion: Its Dubious Impact on American Society* (New York: Basic Books, 1984).

16 Martin Marty, "Righteousness and Grace," *Opening Eyes and Ears: New Connections for Christian Communication*, edited by Kathy Lowe (Geneva: World Council of Churches, 1983), pp. 112-14.

17 Helen Gardner, *Art Through the Ages* (New York: Harcourt, Brace, 1948), p. 684.

18 George Moser, "New Media and the Quality of Life," *Media Development*, 31, 1 (1984), p. 28.

19 Hugo Assmann, *La Iglesia Electronica*, pp. 121-23.

20 Antonio Pasquali, "What UNESCO Hopes to Accomplish in Latin America," *Mass Communication in the Americas: Focus on the New World Information and Communication Order*, edited by Donald Shea and William Jarrett (Milwaukee: University of Wisconsin-Milwaukee, 1985), pp. 10-16.

21 Philip Lee, ed., *Communication for All: New World Information and Communication Order* (Maryknoll., NY: Orbis Books, 1986); Sean MacBride, et. al., *Many Voices, One World: Report by the International Commission for the Study of Communication Problems* (London: UNESCO, 1980).

22 John Bluck, "Communication for Peace and Justice," *Beyond Technology* (Geneva: World Council of Churches, 1984), pp. 64-65.

23 Hugo Assmann, *La Iglesia Electronica*, pp. 25-26, 52-54, 124.

24 Dennis Smith, "The Gospel According to the United States: The Pastoral and Ideological Impact of Evangelical Broadcasting on Central American Christians," *American Evangelicals and the Mass Media*, edited by Quentin Schultze (Grand Rapids: Academic Press, 1990).

25 Robert A. White, "Mass Communication and Culture: Transition to a New Paradigm," *Journal of Communication*, 33 (Summer, 1983), p. 299.

26 Bluck, *Beyond Technology*, pp. 88-89.

27 Ronaldo Munoz, "The Function of the Poor in the Church" *The Poor and the Church* (Concilium 104), edited by Norbert Greinacher and Alois Muller (New York: Seabury Press, 1977), pp. 82-83.

28 Dennis Benson, *The Visible Church* (Nashville: Abingdon Press, 1988).

29 Bluck, *Beyond Technology*, pp. 90-91

CHAPTER EIGHT

(pages 147-155)

MAINTAINING FAITH IDENTITY
IN A TELEVISION CULTURE:
STRATEGIES OF RESPONSE FOR A PEOPLE IN EXILE

1 Wolfgang Yourgrau and Allen Breck, eds., *Cosmology, History and Theology* (New York: Plenum Press, 1977), quoted in Timothy Ferris, *Coming of Age in the Milky Way* (New York: William Marrow, 1988), p. 352.

2 Garrett Green, *Imagining God: Theology and the Religious Imagination* (New York: Harper & Row, 1989), pushes the significance of the imagination in making sense of faith in a provocative, although to what some might consider an extreme, centrality. He writes, "The faithful imagination learns to hear the melody of revelation in the polyphony of scripture. Proclamation can be thought of as singing the scriptural melody so that others may also learn to hear and enjoy it and to join in the singing," p. 151.

3 Jack Solomon, *The Signs of Our Time Semiotics: The Hidden Messages of Environments, Objects, and Cultural Images* (Los Angeles: Jeremy Tarcher, 1988).

4 Ibid., p. 123f.

5 We are indebted to the careful and stirring work of Ralph Klein, *Israel in Exile: A Theological Interpretation* (Philadelphia: Fortress Press, 1979).

6 According to sociologist R. Serge Denisoff, as reported by the Associated Press in the 7 November 1988 edition of *The New Record*, University of Cincinnati newspaper, MTV has climbed to a financial significance second only to sports in the generation of advertising revenues ($100 million a year) with a total income of $8.3 million in 1987, and a head-lock on the success of new groups. "If you're a name group, no problem [getting your video on MTV]. If you're marginal . . . most of the time you're out," p. 10.

7 Solomon writes of these principles of semiotics: "1. Always question the 'commonsense' view of things, because 'common sense' is really 'communal sense': the habitual opinions and perspectives of the tribe. 2. The 'common sense' viewpoint is usually motivated by a cultural interest that manipulates our consciousness for ideological reasons. 3. Cultures tend to conceal their ideologies behind the veil of 'nature,' defining what they do as 'natural' and condemning contrary cultural practices as 'unnatural.' 4. In evaluating any system of cultural practices, one must take into account the interests behind it. 5. We do not perceive our world directly, but view it through the filter of a semiotic code or mythic frame. 6. A sign is a sort of cultural barometer, marking the dynamic movement of social history." *The Signs of Our Times Semiotics*, pp. 123f.

AFTERWARD

(pages 157-160)

1. Popular art and so-called high art in contemporary American culture provide parallel frames of meaning. For many high art has become an access to private visions of the artist. In contrast the popular arts articulate shared political and social symbols. The contrast between the shaping of private and public religious symbols is the subject of my book, *The Electronic Golden Calf: Images, Religion, and the Making of Meaning* (Cambridge: Cowley Publications, 1990).

SELECTED BIBLIOGRAPHY

Allen, Robert, ed. *Channels of Discourse* . Chapel Hill: University of North Carolina Press, 1987.

Armstrong, Ben. *The Electric Church.* New York: Thomas Nelson, 1979.

Bachman, John W. *Media: Wasteland or Wonderland* . Minneapolis: Augsburg, 1984.

Bagdikian, Ben. *The Media Monopoly.* Boston: Beacon, 1983.

Benson, Dennis. *Electric Evangelism.* Nashville: Abingdon Press, 1973.

_____. *The Visible Church.* Nashville: Abington Press, 1988.

Bluck, John. *Beyond Technology: A Christian Critique of the Media.* Geneva: World Council of Churches, 1978.

_____. *Christian Communications Reconsidered.* Geneva: World Council of Churches, 1989.

Boomershine, Thomas. "Biblical Megatrends: Towards a Paradigm for the Interpretation of the Bible in Electronic Media." *SBL 1987 Seminar Papers*: pp. 144-157.

Capra, Fritjof. *The Turning Point: Science, Society and the Rising Culture.* New York: Simon & Schuster, 1982.

Czitrom, D. J. *Media and the American Mind.* Chapel Hill: University of North Carolina Press, 1982.

Ellul, Jacques *The Humiliation of the Word.* Grand Rapids: Eerdmans, 1985.

Enzensberger, Hans *The Consciousness Industry: On Literature, Politics and the Media.* New York: Seabury Press, 1974.

Ewen, Stuart and Elizabeth Ewen. *Channels of Desire: Mass Images and the Shaping of American Consciousness.* New York: McGraw-Hill, 1982.

Fish, Stanley. *Is There a Text in This Class?* Cambridge: Harvard University Press, 1980.

Fore, William. *Image and Impact: How Man Comes Through in the Mass Media.* New York: Friendship Press, 1970.

_____. *Television and Religion: The Shaping of Faith,Values, and Culture*. Minneapolis: Augsburg, 1987.

Frankl, Razelle. *Televagelism: The Marketing of Popular Religion*. Carbondale: Southern Illinois University Press, 1987.

Goethals, Gregor. *The Electronic Golden Calf: Images, Religion, and the Making of Meaning*. Cambridge: Cowley Publications, 1990.

_____. *The TV Ritual: Worship at the Video Altar*. Boston: Beacon Press, 1981.

Himmelstein, Hal. *Television Myth and the American Mind*. New York: Praeger, 1984.

Hoover, Stewart. *The Electronic Giant: A Critique of the Telecommunications Revolution from a Christian Perspective*. Elgin: The Brethren Press, 1982.

_____. *Mass Media Religion: The Social Sources of the Electronic Church*. Newbury Park, CA:Sage, 1988.

Horsfield, Peter. *Religious Television: The American Experience*. New York: Longman, 1984.

Innis, Harold Adams. *The Bias of Communication*. Toronto: University of Toronto Press, 1951.

_____. *Empire and Communication*. Rev. ed. Toronto: University of Toronto Press, 1972.

Jaberg, Gene and Louis Wargo, Jr. *The Video Pencil: Cable Communications for Church and Community*. Washington, D. C.: University Press of America, 1980.

Kraft, Charles. *Communicating the Gospel in God's Way*. Pasadena: William Carey Library, 1983.

Kuhns, William. *The Electronic Gospel: Religion and Media*. New York: Herder and Herder, 1969.

Mander, Jerry. *Four Arguments for the Elimination of Television*. New York: Quill, 1978.

Marty, Martin. *The Improper Opinion: Mass Media and the Christian Faith*. Philadelphia: Westminster Press, 1967.

_____. "Needed: A Christian Interpretation of the Media World." *Lutheran World,* 19: 2 (1972): 105-14.

_____. "Prophecy, Criticism, and Electronic Media." *Media Development* 28: 4 (1981): 30-33.

McDonnell, James and Frances Trampiets, eds. *Communicating Faith in a Technological Age.* Middlegreen, England: St. Paul Publications, 1989.

McLuhan, Marshall. *The Gutenberg Galaxy: The Making of Typographic Man.* Toronto: University of Toronto Press, 1965.

_____. *Understanding Media: The Extensions of Man.* New York:Signet, 1964.

McLuhan, Marshall and Eric McLuhan. *Laws of Media: The New Science.* Toronto: University of Toronto Press, 1988.

McLuhan, Marshall and Bruce Powers. *The Global Village: Transformations in World Life and Media in the 21st Century.* New York: Oxford University Press, 1989.

"The Media and the American Soul." [entire issue] *Luther Theological Seminary Bulletin* 67: 3 (Summer, 1987): articles by Herman Stuempfle, Jr., John Bachman, Robert Lee, John Buchman, Lester Crystal, Marianne Means, Jim Bates and Robert Lee.

Media Development: Journal of the World Association for Christian Communication. London: World Association for Christian Communication. 1953ff.

Meyrowitz, Joshua. *No Sense of Place: The Impact of Electronic Media on Social Behavior.* New York: Oxford, 1985.

Muggeridge, Malcolm. *Christ and the Media.* Grand Rapids: Eerdmans, 1977.

Oberdorfer, Donald. *Electronic Christianity.* Taylor Falls, MN:Brekke, 1982.

Ong, Walter. "Communication Media and the State of Theology." *Cross Currents* 19: 4 (1969): 462-480.

_____. *Orality and Literacy: The Technologizing of the Word.* New York: Methuen, 1982).

_____. *The Presence of the Word: Some Prolegomena for Cultural and Religious History.* New Haven: Yale University Press, 1967.

Owens, Virginia. *The Total Image.* Grand Rapids: Eerdmans, 1980.

Parenti, Michael. *Inventing Reality: The Politics of Mass Media.* New York: St. Martins Press, 1986.

Postman, Neil. *Amusing Ourselves to Death.* New York: Penguin Books, 1985.

Schultze, Quentin, ed. *American Evangelicals and the Mass Media.* Grand Rapids: Zondervan/Academie Press, 1990.

_____. "The Mythos of the Electronic Church." *Critical Studies in Mass Communications* 4 (September, 1987): 245-261.

Solomon, Jack. *The Signs of Our Time Semiotics: The Hidden Messages of Environments, Objects, and Cultural Images.* Los Angeles: Jeremy Tarcher, 1988.

Soukup, Paul. *Communication and Theology: Introduction and Review of the Literature.* London: World Association for Christian Communication, 1983.

"Theology, Education and the Electronic Media." [entire issue] *Religious Education* 82: 2 (Spring, 1987): articles by John Westerhoff, Elizabeth Reed, Robert Liebert and William Kennedy, Everett Parker and William Kennedy, Barbara Hargrave, William Fore, Michael Warren, Tom Driver, Thomas Boomershine, Robert Jenson, Norbert Samuelson, Neil Postman, Hamid Mowland and James Capo.

Waznak, Robert P. "The Church's Response to the Media: Twenty-Five Years After *Inter Mirifica.*" *America* 160:2 (January 21, 1989): 36-40.

White, Robert. "Mass Communication and Culture: Transition to a New Paradigm." *Journal of Communications* 33:3 (1983): 279-301.

_____. "The Word and Electronic Media." *The Way* 20: 1 (1980): 24-35.

Williams, Raymond. *Television: Technology and Cultural Forms.* New York: Schocken Books, 1975.

Winner, Langdon. *Autonomous Technology: Technics-out-of-Control as a Theme in Political Thought.* Cambridge: The MIT Press, 1977.

_____. *The Whale and the Reactor: A Search for Limits in an Age of High Technology.* Chicago: University of Chicago Press, 1986.

INDEX

WHALEPRINTS ™

Production Notes

Design and Artwork
> Cover and Authors' pages designs by Karen Ingle of Penny, Ohlmann, Neiman, Inc., Dayton, Ohio
> Cover photograph (back) by Tom Lehman Concepts, Inc., Dayton, Ohio
> Color separations of cover and endpapers by Accu-Color, Inc., Dayton, Ohio

Type
> Text types are Dutch 11 point on 12 with Helvetica 14 point heads
> Typesetting by Thelma J. Monbarren, United Theological Seminary, Dayton, Ohio, with PageMaker
> Display type by Penny, Ohlman, Neiman, Inc.

Printing and Binding
> Cover: Printed on Georgia 10 point coated one side
> Endpapers: Printed on 17 pound Gilbert Gilclear
> Cover and Endpapers printed by T.L. Krieg Offset, Inc. of Cincinnati, Ohio
> Text: Printed on acid-free 70 pound Cougar Opaque
> Text printing and binding by The Feicke Printing Company, Inc. of Cincinnati, Ohio